PRAISE FOR
The WAY *of* INTERRUPTION

"God breathed, the living Word hovered, darkness ordered, His Creation given life anew. Bill is bringing us back to the old ways, the original ways, with worn leather straps that have carried the burdens of the Church and Her people for two thousand years. It's no surprise it works in the parachurch too. Our nonprofit staff have adopted these practices, and the foundation of the Psalter has brought us spiritual vitality and unity in highly positive ways."

—Matt Hangen,
CEO, Water4.org

"*The Way of Interruption* is itself an interruption. As you read, you will sense that ingrained leadership mindset pushing for some connection to outcomes. As you continue to read, you will feel the brakes being applied to that push, which opens the way to a refreshingly different approach: finding daily transformational moments in simple spiritual practices. I highly commend this shift—from outcomes to practices—to all leaders. Thank you to Bill Simmons for providing both the inspiration and the path to get there."

—Ross Robinson, cofounder/executive leadership coach,
Bold Move International

"Bill interrupts our dichotomy of private and public prayers with a refreshing and practical guide to embrace our spiritual life where many of us spend most of our time—the organization. This remarkable resource will remain close at hand. Thank you, my friend!"

—Mike Mantel, CEO, Living Water International;
author of *Thirsting for Living Water*

"Bill Simmons has given an extraordinary gift to leaders of any organization, bringing ancient wisdom and practices accessibly into the complexities of staff life in today's world, unlocking the transforming potential of God's presence pervading a team. His suggestions are not flashy or complex; they are simply what is needed, like needing clean, cool water in a dry desert. It's not complicated—just necessary and refreshing! *The Way of Interruption* is a timely resource."

—Rev. Bill Haley, executive director, Coracle

"*The Way of Interruption* was a surprise read for me. The concept seemed too simple at first glance. Yet, as I flipped the pages and took the journey with Bill, I recognized that the practices of pause, Psalms, and pray are simple to grasp, but the background, value, and understanding of the practices opened my eyes to something I should do in my personal life, and also consider how to integrate into my business life/company life. Thanks for the fine work, Bill. I'm going to put it into practice."

—Mike Schatz, CDO, partner, 5by5 Agency

"Christian organization leaders struggle with the myth that we control our activities when endless cycles of activities and tasks usually control us. Bill Simmons provides practical steps and tools to interrupt those cycles and restore our right attitude toward Jesus through pause, Psalms, and prayer. We need this, now!"

—Doug Fountain, executive director, Christian Connections for International Health

"*The Way of Interruption* is a book to be experienced, not just read. By embracing its three-step process—pause, Psalm, and prayer—I've found peace amid busyness and clarity amid confusion. I highly recommend this guide, believing the prayers and practices will profoundly impact your life and leadership."

—Peter Greer, president and CEO, HOPE International; coauthor of *Lead with Prayer*

"Even overtly Christian organizations find themselves buried in their work and worries such that our Lord's invitation to abide gets easily obscured. What I love about this book is the way it encourages leaders and their teams to walk time-tested, accessible paths into the peace, wisdom, unity, and joy that can shape everything we do—if we so desire. It's my prayer that the pages of this book shine fresh light on those paths and foster deeper partnerships on the way."

—Seth Cain, rector, Village Church Anglican

"This book delicately and thoughtfully spans the often overwhelming gap between work and prayer. Bill's insights into both the life of the soul with God and the life of work with others—which are, of course, the same—are invaluable and timeless. Take your time with this book, as it is strong, kind, and wise. A quiet and needed blessing."

—Casey Tygrett, spiritual director and author of *The Practice of Remembering: Uncovering the Place of Memories in Our Spiritual Life*

"*The Way of Interruption* speaks directly to a critical question facing today's Christian leaders: Will we continue sacrificing our life with God for organizational success, or will we seek a better path? At Soul Care, we believe that a new path is emerging. We're grateful for Bill's seasoned guidance to help us navigate it. May this book challenge and equip every leader to integrate their deep faith with their work, renewing this essential practice in our time. Well done."

—Mindy Caliguire, CEO, Soul Care; author of *Ignite Your Soul*

"Spiritually stirring, practical, and entertaining—this book serves as an essential road map for leaders seeking to navigate the unique challenges and opportunities that organizations face. This daily guide is an invaluable tool to lead your team through a practice that will help to unite and empower your organization. I highly recommend *The Way of Interruption* to anyone leading a team. By learning the power of taking a pause, your team will breathe new life into their daily work. It will equip you to lead with purpose, foster meaningful relationships, and ultimately make a lasting impact for the Kingdom."

—Seth Colton, president, The Lukens Company

"It's time to rethink how we see interruption. Instead of something to avoid, Bill Simmons shows us the power of embracing interruption through pause, Psalms, and prayer. As we prioritize these spiritual practices in our everyday organizational rhythms, we can avoid what's really distracting us from becoming more like Christ and from following His direction for the ministries we serve."

—Michael Martin, president and CEO, ECFA

The WAY *of* INTERRUPTION

The WAY *of* INTERRUPTION

Spiritual Practice for Organizational Life

Bill Simmons

THE WAY OF INTERRUPTION
Spiritual Practice for Organizational Life

Copyright © 2025 by Bill Simmons

Jacket Design by Abigael Elliott
Cover and Interior Art by David Seth Simmons
Interior Layout and Design by Alice Briggs

ISBNs:
979-8-89165-212-5 *Ebook*
979-8-89165-213-2 *Paperback*
979-8-89165-214-9 *Hardcover*

Published by:
Streamline Books
Kansas City, MO
streamlinebookspublishing.com

DEDICATION

To my grandchildren, through whom God taught me one morning that prayer can be sitting in a chair, reading to your grandchild.

CONTENTS

CONTENTS

CONTENTS

FOREWORD

"Stand at the crossroads, and look, and ask for
the ancient paths, where the good way lies; and
walk in it, and find rest for your souls."
—Jeremiah 6:16 (NRSV)

BILL SIMMONS HAS done a strange and unexpectedly beautiful thing. In the pages that follow, he shares a rather simple idea that turns out to be brilliant precisely because of its simplicity, like a diamond sitting out in the open among many other stones, a diamond that nobody sees because nobody is looking for it. If you're reading this book, keep reading! There's treasure ahead.

Bill has taken ancient wisdom and centuries-old spiritual practices and applied them accessibly to modern organizational life and leadership. He has given organizations a way to unlock the creativity of God in staff life. Granted, seeing communities of Christians attempting to embody the Church's practices and the Bible's timeless wisdom is not all that unusual. But it *is* unusual to see Christian parachurch organizations (nonprofits, local service groups, relief and development organizations, even the staff of a church) do the same. What might God do with an organization that is simply, regularly creating space for God to enter in? What might God do in the life of a staff that interrupts their work and agendas to give up words, and to use the old and new words of others, in prayer?

What is brilliant about the book you're holding is not its fundamental ideas about spiritual interruptions, praying the Psalms, and praying liturgically. It is that these tools are specifically adapted for organizations that may not have yet found a way to bring the simplest, oldest spiritual practices of God's people gently into staff life.

Henri Nouwen gave us the gift of applying the spirituality of the Desert Fathers and Mothers to the modern life of an individual in *The Way of the Heart*. Bill does the same here by connecting tried and true spiritual practices—practices distilled to their essential level by centuries of use—to the organizational life of a team.

My hope for this resource is that leaders and leadership teams would experiment with it in the life of their organizations. My subsequent hope is that God would begin to do strange things: providing a place of quiet amidst noise, a place of peace amidst busyness, a place of discernment amidst many voices, and a place of rest amidst worthy labor. And then, I hope that God would provide even greater power for the mission of the organization seeking to be a part of God's good work in the world.

It's often been said that on the far side of complexity is simplicity. After decades of successful leadership in the Christian business and nonprofit space, on the far side of that complexity, Bill has given us the gift of simplicity in this book. He found a diamond glittering, unexpectedly, among the stones—and now he's giving it to us.

Rev. Bill Haley
Executive Director, Coracle

INTRODUCTION

The Illusion of Control

Tap, tap, TAP.

The startling sound was made by the business end of an AK-47 against my car window. My heart lurched. Headed out for a date, I had just parked along the river road in Kinshasa, Zaire (now the Democratic Republic of the Congo), and here was the Big Bad Wolf at my door—a heavily armed thirteen-year-old in camouflage fatigues.

I should pause to provide a little context. Small-town Tennessee was my first home—but only until I was twelve years old. After becoming disillusioned with the American Dream, my parents answered a call to missionary work with the Presbyterian Church. Their skills in business and education would support the larger work of the Church in Zaire.

We left our comfortable lives behind and moved to a new home across the sea. I attended The American School of Kinshasa, and my middle-Tennessee paradigms quickly fell away in this strange new world. By my senior year of high school, one of my regular goals was to escape the hectic environment of a country and city controlled by the dictator Mobutu Sese Seko—and, as a bonus, to escape my mundane schoolwork. This is what drove me to venture out that fateful evening.

"Get out of the car!"

I jumped to obey the order. Scrambling to get the doors open, I stumbled out of the VW Golf and stood waiting. Then the boy loaded a round of ammunition into the firing chamber.

I began to babble. "Can you ride with us to the US embassy? It's just down the road." I had been taught this was always to be the first response when under threat. Unfortunately, the boy had zero interest in any of the pleas I squeezed out in those precarious few seconds.

My mind was a tumult of panicked thoughts. *This is it. I'm not leaving here alive. Can I rush him? Do I have the guts?* My fear swelled as he started to fumble with his weapon.

"Wait," I blurted. "I have money!"

Child soldiers are neither well paid nor well fed. Praise God, there *was* an envelope of cash in my glove box—meant to pay for dinner, but likely the equivalent of my interrogator's annual wage. Having exhausted myself of the delusion that I could control the situation through negotiation, that money purchased my freedom. Envelope in hand, the young soldier disappeared wordlessly into the shadows and humidity of the night.

Almost forty years later, I still remember those heart-pounding minutes with adrenaline-driven clarity. I had absolutely no idea what would happen next, and I had no real power over the outcome. None. Isn't it strange that we often respond to moments of such total helplessness by working ever harder to avoid them in the future?

When we are confronted by our own utter inability to control what happens to us, it often compounds our belief in a false narrative, the narrative that tells us that we *can* and *should* be in control—that our experiences of powerlessness are just avoidable blips in the normal pattern where we *are* in control. So we resolve to avoid those irritating moments that disrupt the illusion of control in the future, and, unchecked, the false narrative swells and seeps into other areas of our lives.

The Freedom of Relinquishing Control and Embracing a System

You may not find yourself held at gunpoint, but I know you understand what I mean: You experience those frustrating, eye-opening moments of powerlessness from time to time when your flight is delayed, or a beloved staff member decides to move on, or your child catches the flu on the worst possible day. You just cannot control everything. Not in your personal life, your family, your spiritual life, or your organization. And any attempt to do so will drive you crazy.

As the CEO of a Christian nonprofit, I've been on a journey over the last decade and a half, one of yielding my control to God both in my private life and in my leadership and direction of the organization. It has been so freeing to loosen my grip on that false story, the story that I can and should steer the ship regarding every single aspect of my life and work. As my spiritual director once pointed out, the more I've grown in releasing control, the more God has drawn me to lean on the freeing structure of *practice*—routines, traditions, and procedures.

For example, my organization uses the Carver Model system of board governance.[1] I tell fellow CEOs all the time that in using this system, with its abundance of policies (laws and rules, if you will), I have experienced more freedom and clarity as a leader than ever before in my previous stints as a CEO. I am scaffolded in my work; my burden has been lightened, and my hands freed up. With firm guidelines and walls around me, provided by an outside source rather than generated and controlled by me, I can see and move unencumbered. I believe this is the sort of liberty God intended when he gave the law to the people of Israel: freedom within obedience and order. It may be the opposite of control, but it feels like true freedom.

When CEOs Are Expected to Be Pastors: The Freedom of an Ancient Way

If you are a leader or CEO of a Christian organization, you're familiar with a heightened level of pressure in your role; you're implicitly, or perhaps explicitly, expected to bring a pastor's heart and vision into the life of the organization. The faith life of your team while at work, impossibly enough, is yet another thing you are supposed to control. I have felt this pressure for my entire career. At times, I was burdened by the need to drum up and sustain an enthusiastic spiritual culture throughout the organization, and when I led retreats, I knew I was expected to cultivate a life-changing, old-time revival atmosphere. These expectations can manifest in a variety of ways, adding to what is already a difficult and weighty job: guiding an organization, its people, and its mission.

Recently, I laid it all down. The burden the world had placed on me to create, drive, develop, and control a spiritual corporate culture, I laid down at the feet of Christ. In return, I received clarity about the easy and light burden Jesus returned to me in its stead. My efforts to control were yielded up, and I discovered the freedom that comes from simply leaning into old ways.

God has been undoing the illusion of control in my life and career, which had gathered like moss through events, including that interrupted date night all those years ago. These are sloughing off and dissipating in the morning sun, in the radiance of the glory of a transcendent God. This project is the unfolding of that clarity and what I believe God wants this leader to do *less* of so that *he* may do more. Perhaps you will find it is true for you, too.

OVERVIEW

THIS BOOK WAS designed to provide you with a rhythm of corporate prayers and spiritual practices for use within your organizational setting, prayers and practices that are grounded in the ancient ways of God's Church. I pray this steady structure will free you from *your* burden of generating, reinventing, and controlling the spiritual culture of your organization, as it has done for me and my team.

The book is divided into three sections: practices, a Psalter[2] guide, and prayers and liturgies. Each section contains an introduction to and reflection on the respective tool, as well as practical guidance for use.

The first section describes the three simple practices my organization has adopted into our corporate rhythms and organizational life, used one after the other at the beginning of every meeting.

The Practices of the Way of Interruption Are:

1. Pause.
2. Psalms.
3. Pray.

These practices may be adapted however you see fit in your work setting.

The second section is a Psalter guide, a calendar of readings for each workday of the year, which can be used during the second of the three practices described. This Psalter guide is meant to create a unified sharing of Scripture across an organization as God speaks in his own way to all involved. On page 63 you will find a QR code to access the daily guide for yourself or for others in your organization.

Lastly, the compilation of liturgical prayers for various activities and moments in organizational life can be used to bring people together in one voice around these shared experiences. There are so many rituals of organizational life, from onboarding a new staff member to launching a new project to kicking off a board meeting. Each of these moments provides an opportunity to bring our worlds and words together in the unity of shared practices. The liturgical prayers in this book, many of them contributed by CEOs and leaders of parachurch ministries around the world, provide the perfect place to experience and cultivate shared practices.

Together, these practices and prayers can bring an organization's diversity of individuals together and move the team toward unity. They are designed to be accessible to all, regardless of individual church or denominational background.

I pray these practices will allow you, too, to release control, lighten your load, and embrace the freedom of following a travel-worn path.

PRACTICES

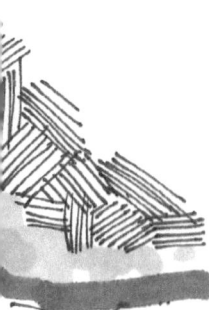

The NECESSITY *of* INTERRUPTION

"There is no music in a rest, but there is the making of music in it."
—John Ruskin[3]

The Mountain

It was a bright July day, clouds creeping across a Microsoft Windows wallpaper–blue sky. I climbed out of the car, paused, and contemplated the challenge ahead: the daunting 13,167-foot summit of Mount Wheeler.

Sure, Wheeler isn't the tallest mountain in the Sangre de Cristo Mountains (named for Christ's blood after a crimson sunset 300 years ago). I was already in the deserted parking lot of a ski resort at 9,300 feet; what was 4,000 feet more? I was in good shape and had even just completed my first half-marathon a few weeks earlier. So what if the climb ahead would cover steep, rocky terrain, with the majority of the mountain's craggy height suddenly spurting upwards during the last three miles? So what if I'd taken no time to acclimate to the elevation after the trip from my placidly sea-level South Carolina home? Piece of cake.

I was sick as a dog before I was halfway up. Vengeful altitude sickness loves to pounce on a foolish novice, and so I was forced to stop, rest, and contemplate the lessons of Icarus every hundred yards or so. My head swam, my stomach lurched, and each step forward became an exertion of the will. A woman, at least ten years my elder, breezed past with an airy hello and the tinkling click of hiking poles. A ten-year-old girl scrambled over rocks, face shining with triumph as she followed her family back down after their successful climb. Elevation had sapped my strength, and embarrassment and shame now threatened to steal my resolve as well. Lord knows why I kept going. Four excruciating hours later, I finally reached the summit.

Breathing the clear air for a moment, I waited for my heart to settle. An unkindness of ravens descended to feast on a patch of snow nearby, and I could see a gray haze of rain approaching across the range, accompanied by low growls of thunder. I didn't linger long.

Descending over the ankle-turning rocks and boulders, I was again overwhelmed by dizziness and nausea so intense that I had visions of collapsing, of being hoisted by a helicopter rescue team off the mountain or carried down on a gurney like an injured soldier. Gasping for air at an elbow-sharp bend in the path, I pulled a small wooden cross from my pocket, a gift from a friend, and my desperation pushed me into an out-of-character act: I clutched the cross and prayed aloud.

"Lord, help me off this mountain. I don't want to be taken off in a helicopter, and I don't want to be caught in a lightning storm. Lord, come to my assistance; make haste to help me."

My eyes opened, and the moment was interrupted. A female bighorn sheep, which had been nowhere in sight a heartbeat earlier, quietly moved in front of me. She walked down the path ahead of me a short distance, climbed up on a rock at the path's edge, and watched. I felt a sigh in my soul as everything came back into focus. I locked eyes with that sheep and stood in a silence that felt like a reply: "It will be okay; you'll make it down." It was God's "I haven't forgotten you" message to me. I crept past her and made it back to the car alive.

Interruptions

I don't know if God *made* that sheep appear right when I opened my eyes, but I do know God *used* her—or at least, the symbol of her—to reassure me of his presence as the Good Shepherd. Absorbed as I was by the rocks in my path, by my misery, by my concentration on each next step, what I needed right then was an interruption. I needed to be forced to stand still, to turn my face outwards and upwards, to breathe and remember that something existed beyond my spinning head, my catastrophic thinking, and the crunch of my feet along the trail. Pausing for interruption has the power to reorient us when we need it most. God was orienting me to interruption by speaking to me through this beautiful creature that appeared as if through a portal from another world and onto the path ahead.

Think of that movie trope where a character descending into hysteria is "snapped out of it" by a helpful slap in the face and the resulting moment of breathless shock. Recall the last time you were shaken out of your absorption with daily tasks and into smiling silence by a child's sticky kiss or a loving text message. Imagine the score of Vivaldi's "Spring," unpunctuated by rest symbols, gnarled into a continuous chaos of sound without breath, without pause. We are oriented, shaped, and propelled by the interruptions woven into our lives.

The Ripples

As the CEO of an international organization that is over 118 years old, my role forms a huge part of what I do and who I am. It did not take long before my encounter with the sheep and my personal experience of that reorienting moment set me wondering—what could it look like for these life-giving interruptions to be integrated into the rhythms of an organization? The seed of this book had been planted, and a few days later, it would be watered and take root in an unexpected place—a monastery in the desert.

Christ in the Desert

In the great western state of New Mexico, you can find places that exist outside of time and space. These are places where the body, mind, and soul can still reach and speak to us in ways that we rarely experience when we are elbow-deep in the hubbub of our modern lives.

Following my precipitous encounter with God and his ewe on Mount Wheeler, I headed north from Santa Fe accompanied by my friend Reverend Bill Haley. Sixteen miles outside the small town of Abiquiu, there is a left turn off the highway onto a sandy desert road. The road isn't treacherous, but it does run around narrow, guardrail-free bends that overlook the flowing Rio Chama. The river has cut into the land over the centuries, splitting the earth into a stark valley with steep desert cliffs standing watch over the wide-open space. It is the land of Georgia O'Keeffe, whose Ghost Ranch is only ten minutes back down the paved road.

Almost an hour after you leave the pavement behind, the desert cliffs draw closer to each other, pinching the road toward the river, and a hand-carved wooden sign emerges around the bend: "Peace— Monastery of Christ in the Desert, Dead End Road Ahead." The Abbot says it is the most remote monastery in the Western Hemisphere, and I felt that remoteness in my bones when we arrived. The monks of Christ in the Desert open their doors to those seeking sojourn and retreat from the restless world. Bill and I prayed in the car before entering those doors and agreed to maintain silence, as the monks do, throughout our visit.

I can't begin to share the fullness of what I learned in the depths of my heart during my time at the monastery. As Henri Nouwen says in *The Way of the Heart*,

> The soul, in its desire to say many things, dissipates its remembrance of God through the door of speech, even though everything it says may be good. Thereafter, the intellect, though lacking appropriate ideas, pours out a welter of confused thoughts to anyone it meets, as it no longer has the Holy Spirit to keep its understanding from fantasy. Ideas of value always shun verbosity, being foreign to confusion and fantasy. *Timely silence, then, is precious, for it is nothing less than the mother of wisest thoughts.*[4]

With that acknowledgment, I will endeavor here to share, without verbosity, my most treasured desert learning, this new understanding of *the way of interruption* that has forever changed my life (and, perhaps, the life of my organization).

The Weaving of Work and Worship

Seven times a day, the monks of Christ in the Desert come to the chapel to observe the Liturgy of the Hours, sometimes called the Divine Office. The primary forms observed date back to the late 400s during the time of Saint Benedict,[5] but the practice at the heart of the offices, the praying of the Psalms, is downright ancient. Daily Psalm prayers are rooted in historic Jewish practice; even Jesus himself would surely have whispered David's laments and exaltations morning and night while growing up in Galilee. The liturgical practice of the Temple has included the Psalms since as far back as the First Temple Period, which ended in 586 BC. For today's monks, the eight liturgies of the hours form a pattern lived out between four o'clock in the morning and seven o'clock in the evening every single day.

Like me and like you, these monastics have work to do. They run their property, cook, farm, manage their gift shop, pay bills ... the list goes on. In spite of their distinctive black cloth habits, their daily lives are made up of the same mundane routines found in the greater world outside. Even in a monastery, there is no true retreat from *work*. Yet amidst the constant and never-ending stream of tasks, they interrupt that work eight times a day, every day, 365 days a year. It matters not the season nor the importance of the to-do list; when the bell rings, work is set aside, and they return to the chapel and the Psalms.

Some might think that this ancient liturgical practice could become monotonous, and perhaps even the monks themselves would agree from time to time. But that is not the point. The point is that *they have oriented their lives to this interruption*. It is an interruption aimed at conforming the mind, body, and spirit to the shape of the divine. As Paul writes in Philippians 2:9–11,

"Therefore, God elevated him to the place of highest honor and gave him the name above all other names, that at the name of Jesus, every knee should bow, in heaven and on earth and under the earth, and every tongue declare that Jesus Christ is Lord, to the glory of God the Father."

When the whole world arrives at this moment, in the presence of Jesus, everyone will bow; everyone will conform to the shape of a life bent in praise. Paul doesn't describe this as something we *decide* to do or not do. Like sunflowers who unknowingly lift their faces to follow the sun's progress across the sky, we will simply find ourselves on our knees with our faces lifted toward Christ.

Psalm 46 contains a similar verse that has become a meme for quiet contemplation on God: "Be still, and know that I am God." I think this is often misunderstood. The preceding verses say,

> Come, see the glorious works of the Lord:
> See how he brings destruction upon the world.
> He causes wars to end throughout the earth.
> He breaks the bow and snaps the spear;
> he burns the shields with fire.

This passage certainly does not conjure up quiet images of flowing streams and quiet benches. God is speaking a command to the armies, whose bows and spears are broken, shields crumbling to ash on the battlefield. Be still! And know that I am God. His presence brings armies to a halt, and all must obey his command.

Our posture as humans toward God, when faced with his realness, is always awe that knocks us to our knees. Throughout Scripture, we see people encounter God and his emissaries, and the almost universal response is to bow to the ground. In this modern world, we have hidden God behind a curtain for so long that most days, we forget he is there at all. We lead our lives under the control of the laws of the universe and not the God of the universe. If we can only make it a practice to peek behind the curtain, over and over throughout the day, catching glimpses of the God who is, our lives will be different. This glimpse behind the curtain is what I observed in the desert monastery.

The monastic approach to the liturgy takes worship as a natural posture, a positioning toward the only thing that truly matters. The point is not really what each person "gets" from observing the liturgy.

It is not about our effort or even, ultimately, our betterment. As I sat listening, praying, and singing the Psalms with these men, I began to see that the liturgical interruptions in their days were all about God and not at all about them. They seemed to accept that there was indeed a God, thinly veiled but ever present. God deserves worship and praise irrespective of how we feel or whether we are able to experience something that changes us. The sunflowers don't worry about whether they're photosynthesizing or not; they are simply, irresistibly drawn toward the sun because it is the sun.

During my time at Christ in the Desert, I started to wonder if the monks were truly interrupting their work in order to pray or if it was the prayers that were being temporarily suspended while they turned to their work. Life and worship are woven so seamlessly together there that the question almost seemed to be its own answer. Like the crests and troughs of a great sea's waves, work and worship interrupt one another in a rhythm that creates a coherent, good, and right whole.

Humanity places a high value on "getting things done." You've experienced this; you experience it every day, wherever you labor. The to-do list never gets fully checked off, does it? And those projects and deadlines seem so easily to swell, to loom, to become insurmountable. We focus desperately on the rocks at our feet and forget to catch our breath, to keep an eye out for any symbolically stirring sheep God might shoo our way, to allow for reorienting interruption, a sacred pause.

What would a workplace look like if it ground to a halt over and over again each day, rhythmically pausing for silence, Psalms, and prayer? What if these ancient practices that emerged with the Desert Fathers from Egypt almost two thousand years ago were applied to the patterns of my own life and to the life of an organization?

That is what I returned from the monastery determined to discover. Reflecting on the *essential* parts of those practices that might apply in my context, I set out to adopt practices that could be integrated into the hurried patterns of organizational life. As we incorporated these intentional, reorienting ways of interruption into our culture, the shape of our team and work began to change. Much of what has happened is, was, and will be mysterious because it lives in the transcendent space that seems out of reach to so many in our modern age.

Like the monks at Christ in the Desert, we continue to observe our practices of interruption at our organization, not for our own sakes, but simply to bend the knees of our hearts and minds toward our God, who is the reason for all our boundless activity. What long-term good will come of regularly interrupted work and the reminder that God is among us and that each of our team members is an icon of the *imago dei*, the image of God? I can't say. It isn't *for* our own long-term good that we observe these practices. Our practices permit us to redeem time and enable us to be present to each other in a way Jesus modeled. We breathe the Scriptures out into the world and pray again for God's timely assistance. These practices are not aimed at us but instead are aimed at our Creator and Redeemer. That is what I hope this book reveals to you.

My Hopes for You, for Me, and for Us All

The practices described in the pages to come are meant to be interruptions at the beginning of every meeting at your organization, in succession: pause, read a Psalm, then pray. As the monastics turn their faces to God throughout the day, the practices are meant to halt, reset, and reorient the flow of your organizational life—again and again.

I left that quiet desert monastery having encountered a glimpse of our eternal God and Father in the cloister of that desert canyon. I left intent on interrupting the flow of my life, on reorienting myself toward Christ daily in both my inhales and my exhales. Perhaps these interruptions would allow me to peer through the Narnian wardrobe beyond my present world and into the world beyond. And on some days, I might even see the great lion himself, Aslan, far off in the distance. Maybe, just maybe.

Lord, let it be so.

PAUSE

"The first service that one owes to others in the fellowship
consists in listening to them. Just as love to God begins
with listening to his Word, so the beginning of love
for the brethren is learning to listen to them."
—Dietrich Bonhoeffer[6]

Modern Barriers to Presence

What distracts you from fully *paying attention*? For me, it's often my
handy-dandy smartphone—nothing rare about that, I know. It's such
a convenient tool, and such a noisy, shiny one at that, and it gets in
the way of my very real human relationships far too often.

One of my sons has taken an unusual step in comparison to his
millennial peers. He recently abandoned the modern smartphone
and purchased something called a Light Phone.[7] It's about the size
of a credit card and not much thicker than a pencil. The screen

looks like a Kindle book screen, and on the whole, it is confusingly unlike anything we now think of as a phone. He regularly gets stares while walking down the street, as people can't figure out what he is holding to his ear! The Light Phone does two things: it makes phone calls, and it sends and receives text messages. Its advertising asserts that it is "designed to be used as little as possible." How refreshing. (Disclaimer: no, I am not being paid for this praise. Bear with me, I have a point.)

Without placing all the blame squarely on smartphones and their incessant cries for our attention and mental investment, being present *is* one of the greatest challenges to human relationships today. Modern life is a harried and hurried thing. We are constantly multitasking; our minds are pulled in one hundred different directions. Within the tumult, is it any wonder that it takes a colossal effort to stop, stand still, and turn our attention—lovingly, fully, respectfully—to the human standing before us?

The challenge is only compounded in organizational settings, where team members today wade through flurries of back-to-back meetings with little time to catch their breath—and where human contact is so often limited to the sterile, alienating barrier of a two-dimensional video conferencing screen. We rush from one agenda to another, managing multiple computer monitors while our inboxes ping and our smartphones buzz with notifications in the background. This creates a frenetic sea of activity where team members are always in a hurry and are often still processing one meeting when, lo and behold, they have to scurry off to the next.

Paying full attention (or, as Bonhoeffer suggests, "learning to listen") to another person is a dying art. I think it is one of the keys to living fully in this world, but it's a rare commodity in many organizational cultures. It is a principle worth fighting for, and one that Jesus of Nazareth modeled as he walked the dusty roads of Galilee.

Subway Pressure

Once, on a trip to New York, I stayed on Long Island but attended meetings every day in Manhattan. The fastest and most direct way into the city was the subway, so each day, I waited on the distinctly scented platform during the early morning rush, withstanding the crush of people as the car slid to a stop and inserting myself into the bare slip of space revealed once its doors opened. Hardy subway riders know that as you approach this blob of humanity, it will slowly give way and absorb you like an amoeba. You grasp for a handhold, the doors slide closed, and you are held upright by the press of people around you.

Savvy folks also know to make sure they have valuables in front pockets and wear their backpack as a "frontpack." I'm sure you've heard at least one legend of unwitting travelers having bags cut open or pockets picked in these transit cars. After all, how would a person know anyone had ever done such a thing from within the sardine tin? Recalling those crammed subway cars, I still feel a visceral, lung-tightening sensation of pressure.

The eighth chapter of Luke's Gospel tells us that Jesus, too, has been in the sardine tin—caught in the push and pull of a disorienting crowd. Imagine the hubbub of voices, the sea of faces, hands reaching out in supplication from all sides. A leader named Jairus fights his way through to beg Jesus to heal his sick daughter, and Jesus begins to make his way toward the little girl. It must have been like wading through chin-high mud—the end of verse 42 says, "The crowds almost crushed him."

In the middle of this maelstrom, Jesus pauses and says, "Someone touched me; power has gone out of me." Peter is nonplussed: "Master, the people are crowding and pressing against you."[8] In Mark's account, the disciples reply, "You see the people crowding against you, and yet you can ask, 'Who touched me?'"[9] They cannot imagine that there is any way that *anyone* might know the answer to that question.

If you know this story, you know that a woman who had been bleeding for twelve years brushed her hand against his cloak and was healed by her faith. As amazing a miracle as this is, I've often wondered how Jesus recognized that it had happened at all. Most people would point to his divine nature as an answer, but I'd suggest we might look to his human side for an explanation as well.

Writer, theologian, and philosopher Dallas Willard writes that Jesus "is the smartest man who ever lived."[10] Similarly, I believe he was the most fully present human ever to walk this planet. Here he was in the midst of this wild throng of people, but I believe he was *paying attention* to each of them, that he was ever attuned to the needs and emotions of those around him. He perceives this woman. He is hyperaware of all the humans before him, and somewhere at the bottom of the robes and feet of this crowd is a person he knows is there but whom he cannot see.

WWJD?

Jesus was seemingly never in a hurry. He scolded the disciples for rebuffing the children,[11] and when he passed through Jericho, he stopped his journey to have dinner with Zacchaeus.[12] In the story above, the crowd wants to hurry Jesus to Jairus's daughter, but even in this life-and-death situation, he pauses to be present to the woman who touched him.

Jesus knew that each person had dignity. He knew that they were intrinsically worth his time. Dignity is from the Latin word *dignus*, which means "worth." The origin of that worth lies in another Latin phrase, *imago dei*, the image of God. Inside each person is the Creator's image, and Jesus could see his Father in every person he met.

We are expected to function like Jesus in our organizations, fully acknowledging and respecting the *imago dei* of each person we encounter daily. How can we do so in an age of distraction? In the way of interruption, it is by practicing a simple ritual of pausing.

How to Pause

I recommend practicing pause at the beginning of every single meeting throughout your workday—opening each call or gathering with a moment of quiet in which you prepare to give your full attention to the worthy people in front of you.

To show up well to the *imago dei* in others, we must acknowledge those things that distract us. If your phone is on your desk, set it aside (or even better, turn it off). If you operate with multiple monitors or split screens, make the video meeting screen the only one you see. When using a video meeting platform like Zoom, stay on speaker view. Whatever you need to do to remove distractions, do it. The point of doing these things is not to curb our behaviors but to honor the other people with whom we are meeting.

I have been on Zoom calls on more than one occasion where the other person is clearly looking down at their phone or responding to emails throughout the meeting. This choice conveys that whoever is speaking is not worthy of attention—and no one relishes being ignored or dismissed.

Inattention is the ultimate unkindness, albeit one that is simple to correct. A human soul is a wondrous thing, and after a pause and some mindful breaths, that reality is all the more obvious and convicting—and it changes how we choose to react to whatever distracts us from honoring and focusing on the people in front of us. If you are a leader, you might take an inventory among your team members about what distracts them most and what gets in the way of being fully present. You can build an internal team covenant to avoid, eliminate, or control those things that distract you from honoring the image of God in others.

In our organization, we lay aside our distractions and begin each meeting with a moment of quiet. Whatever we have just hurried from, whether personal or professional, our first act is always to catch our breath collectively.

On many highways around the world, there are signs reading "Scenic Overlook Ahead." Most of these are missed by passing cars in an anxious hurry to get to the next destination. The practice of pausing is a lot like pulling off the highway, putting the car in park, and taking a moment to breathe the fresh air and take in the amazing view. Waving at the scenic overlook from the car or craning one's neck to catch a cheap glimpse cannot replace the moment of pausing and stopping at the overlook.

Our agendas and our work are their own form of that collective hurry of traffic that "must" get to where it is going. The monks in the desert remind us that the pause—pulling the metaphorical car off the road—is an essential act, maybe even more important than the destination.

Breathing

We encourage our leaders to start every meeting with between thirty seconds and three minutes of pause. We begin by taking slow, deep breaths. This takes the focus off whatever meeting just ended and all the things that are on the to-do list. Pausing brings us back into our bodies from our wandering minds.

There is plenty of research about the positive impact of slow, deep breathing.[13] In 2018 a team of neuroscientists wrote that the effects of slow breathing were "increased comfort, relaxation, pleasantness, vigor and alertness, and reduced symptoms of arousal, anxiety, depression, anger, and confusion."[14] Sounds like a great way to start a meeting.

My wife often tells our two-year-old granddaughter, when she is on the verge of a meltdown, "Take three deep breaths." That simple action can move a toddler from demanding something one moment to quietly asking for it the next. As adults, we may have more immediate self-control now than we did when we were two, but we are still deeply affected by our interactions and emotions throughout the day. Yet, how rare is it in an organization for us to slow things down enough for people to take a deep breath? Too many leaders place the strategy and tactics that "must get done" above how team members show up. What would happen if you slowed down consistently?

In my organization, if we only have thirty seconds, we take three deep breaths; but the longer you choose to pause, the better. Having done this hundreds of times, I have found that third breath to be the one where my shoulders relax, and I can feel tension leave my body. I know it is only an experiment with one participant, so try it out for yourself and see what your results are.

Three minutes can seem an interminable length in our fast-paced world, but when we take that amount of time to really come to a pause, our presence changes. As we breathe more slowly and catch up to ourselves, we also invite the meeting participants to consider moving even deeper into the practice of pausing.

Releasing

We can begin with what Paul encourages us to do: "Take every thought captive."[15] This verse is often used when people talk about thoughts that lead to temptation or sin, but I'd like to point out that it does say *every thought*: thoughts about the previous meeting's task list, what we're having for lunch, what we want to say next. All the action items racing in our minds, the frustrations with another team member, the pressure to achieve—these and so many others are floating behind the scenes when people come into a meeting. We all need a moment to let those thoughts come into view, slowly release them, and let them float away to be dealt with at an appropriate moment elsewhere during the day.

Need a script for encouraging your team to take this step? When I lead this practice, I sometimes say, "Now take every thought captive. Identify those things in your mind that are distracting you from being present in this meeting and release them back to God's control. Let them drift away, if only for this moment."

The distractions of the day, personal or professional, can overwhelm our minds and prevent us from showing up well to the people around us. Letting our wild mental scrabbling go feels like the relief that comes from a good, deep sigh.

Recollecting

Next, we take a moment to *recollect ourselves*. People often say, "I need a moment to collect my thoughts," but have you ever heard someone say, "I need to recollect myself"? Me neither. As I spent time reflecting and reading about how to become more present, I uncovered this concept of *recollection*. It's a vital idea, especially in organizations that aim to change the world and lives for the kingdom of God.

A quick lookup of this word yields the following: *To remember or become aware of one's purpose, intention, or situation, especially after a momentary interruption, diversion, or distraction; to become recomposed.*

In his little book, *The Practice of the Presence of God*, the French monk Brother Lawrence draws our attention to this practically. Brother Lawrence says, "Make it your study, before taking up any task, to look to God, be it only for a moment, as also when you are engaged thereon, and lastly when you have performed the same."[16] Lawrence encourages us toward an attitude that brings us back to God as we begin our work and or agendas. This recollection, however brief, realigns us with God and his purposes. Thomas Merton writes, "Recollection consists of listening for God's will."[17] God's will and our purpose are one. The recollection of that purpose enables us to put down whatever we have picked up throughout the day, whatever may have gotten in the way of that divine calling.

Organizational calendars are a constant and all-encompassing stream of events and tasks that must be done. We need to be reminded, frequently and powerfully, of our purpose in the midst of the busywork. This enables us to recall our core aims, team values, commitment to one another, and most of all, our aim of dignifying the people we are in a (real or virtual) room with at any given moment.

Just Do It

Pausing is one of the most uncomplicated things we do in our organization, but it is certainly among the most important. Our missions are too important to ignore the people right in front of us. Jesus was on a mission to see Jairus's daughter, and he was fully on that path. But that focus, that agenda, did not detract from his practice of being present to the people around him in any given moment. If he had not interrupted his agenda and paused to recognize the dignity of this woman, we would never have known her story.

When you have a meeting—and I mean any and every meeting— start by taking thirty seconds (*or be ambitious and take the whole three minutes!*) to pause. Invite everyone in your meeting, whether there are thirty people or only two, to do the same. We are all adrift in the river of hurry in our modern age. Leaders like you can throw an anchor to the shore of recollection so that we might regain our own dignity and be able to sit fully present to the *imago dei* in others. I promise it will be worth it.

Summary—The Way of Interruption—Pause

How to pause as a team:

1. Remove distractions.

2. Breathe—deeply, slowly, and silently.

3. Take every thought captive.

4. Recollect yourself.

PSALMS

"Though all Scripture, both old and new, is divinely inspired
and has its use in teaching, as we read in Scripture itself, yet the
Book of Psalms, like a garden enclosing the fruits of all the other
books, produces its fruits in song, and in the process of singing
brings forth its own special fruits to take their place beside them.
The Psalms seem to me to be like a mirror, in which the person
using them can see himself, and the stirrings of his own heart; he
can recite them against the background of his own emotions."
—Athanasius[18]

World-Shaped, God-Shaped

We live in a *me, me, me* society. Marketing campaigns shout that we
deserve the best. Social media croons to our egos. Popular music and
movies roar that we can be whatever we want to be if we just follow
our hearts, never mind the cost. We are born selfish, and the world
preys on our lesser selves. Like a windswept tree on a hillside, our

life slowly bends into the shape of this egocentric world we navigate daily. Breaking out of that mold is an ongoing struggle and not one for the faint of heart.

Romans 12:2 urges us: "Do not conform to the pattern of this world, but be transformed by the renewing of your mind." Easier said than done. We could apply the world's methodology to attaining this, expending our own energy and willpower in an attempt to change ourselves for the better, but we will find ourselves on a path that is self-generating and not at all sustainable. I have spent a lot of time trying to force my life into a godly shape all on my own without much success. But just as we can be warped by the world through sheer exposure, we can be shaped into God's image too—through choosing to be immersed in his presence, and by placing his words on our tongues.

Over twenty years of my career were spent leading Christian retail bookstore chains with locations across the United States. This gave me access to books on every topic imaginable relating to the Christian life. I still love books—heck, I'm sitting here writing this one—but they are only signposts. You certainly cannot study yourself to sainthood. However, all the answers we are looking for can be found in the most ancient of tomes, the Bible. When it comes to resisting the pattern of this world, we really need look no further. I can hear the revivalist saying, "It's in this holy book. God said it, that settles it." Like most sayings like this, there is a seed of truth inside.

In his book *The Way of the Heart*, Henri Nouwen discusses short prayers as part of our daily practice: "Our choice of words depends on our needs and the circumstances of the moment, *but it is best to use words from Scripture.*"[19] In the New Mexico desert monastery, I turned to the same source for shaping my own prayers, and to find a way of being truly at odds with the pattern of the world.

God-Breathed

In Paul's second letter to Timothy, chapter 3:16, he tells Timothy, "All Scripture is God-breathed." The Greek word is *theopneustos*—*theo-*, or God, and *-pneustos*, having to do with breath or wind, like the breath that formed Adam out of dust, the breath in our lungs today. Scripture is God-breathed, as are we, and we are called to breathe out Scripture together too.

Monks live two kinds of lives. Before my journey to a monastery, I imagined them sitting quietly, reflecting, and praying alone. They *do* live a private life of personal prayer and devotion, but that is not the main thing. Most of their spiritual and daily lives are spent in community with their fellow monastics. Eight times a day, they enter the chapel to quietly chant Scripture aloud—together.

After entering the chapel, the monks make their way to the benches on either side of the altar, sitting in old wooden pews facing each other. The cantor begins the prayers, and the monks on one side of the chapel quietly chant a verse while the others listen. Then, those on the other side grab onto the last word chanted and pick up the next verse. Back and forth it goes, like the heaving sighs of inhales and exhales, Scripture breathed out into the world through their voices.

I grew up in a mainline Protestant tradition and attended a nondenominational church for many years as an adult. In spite of all my apparent churching, my short stay at the monastery exposed me to more Scripture—namely, the Psalms—spoken out loud than I had heard in all my years prior. It was an absolute immersion in the very real sound of God's Word, a strange and shaping kind of baptism.

An Ancient Path as Spiritual Formation

In organizations like the one I am honored to steward, we are surrounded by a diverse group of people whose practices and formation on a given Sunday are all quite different. So what is the role of spiritual formation in an organization composed of this kind of diversity?

I've come to believe that it is our job to ensure that the work that we do together can be conformed to the image of God. Spiritual formation in the workplace should enable our work and team to be God-shaped. We are not forming doctrine or teaching per se. Instead, it is my view that we want to bring God into our space and work so that we, as a community of believers, are doing kingdom work together in a way that honors and proclaims the gospel.

To that end, I am convinced that in order to work for God's glory we must turn our hearts toward God *together* and *regularly*, breathing out Scripture as the monks do, letting God shape our work for the day. As I've mentioned in previous chapters, the pressure to create this kind of spiritual culture, shepherding those they lead, can be entirely overwhelming for organizational leaders. Thankfully we have been given a path we can follow.

Psalms are an ancient way of praying, and some individual Psalms are indeed ancient in themselves. Psalm 90 begins, "Lord, through all generations, you have been our home. Before the mountains were born, before you gave birth to the earth and the world, from beginning to end, you are God." This Psalm is attributed to Moses, who lived around 1400 BC. Daily, around the world, millions of Christians of all denominations pray through the Psalms, individually and collectively—just like the brothers at Christ in the Desert.

The monks lead us back to the ancient way. Jeremiah 6:16 says,

"Stand at the crossroads and look;
ask for the ancient paths,

ask where the good way is, and walk in it,
and you will find rest for your souls."

Author and theologian Tom Wright urges us to enter this very kind
of formation and transformation. He says that regularly praying the
Psalms can change how we understand who, when, and what we are:
"The Psalms will gently but firmly transform our understandings.
They do this so that we may be changed, transformed, so that we
look at the world, one another, and ourselves in a radically different
way ... God's way."[20]

This releases organizational leaders from the expectation that they
will shape and form their teams and staff. Instead, Scripture, including
Psalms, brought alive by God, will transform people as God wills and
works in and through these living words.

Practice the Psalms

This good way, the ancient path that I feel called to share with you,
is the breathing out of Psalms together in our organizations. I am
in no way diminishing any other parts of Scripture. But what is the
most practical and accessible Scripture we can incorporate into an
organizational practice? I think it is the Psalms. Psalms have served
as communal prayers for Jewish and Christian communities for hundreds of years. Praying the Psalms creates a monastic-like rhythm in
our days. This well-worn and time-tested path frees leaders from the
felt need to innovate and to instead stand on the shoulders of those
great saints who have come before us.

In ecumenical organizations, the Psalms can bring diverse groups
of people together. I have never heard of a church that split over
Psalm 23, nor have I read of a schism caused by discussing Psalm 19.
There are other places in Scripture where people may take nuanced

stances or even divisive ones, but the Psalms are a place of poetry and agreement.

In my organization, directly after taking a moment to pause at the beginning of a meeting, we pray a Psalm. Every meeting I have during the day starts this way. We interrupt our own hurry and urgency and are stilled and oriented by a moment of quiet, and then we join together to turn our faces to God and read the ancient words of David or Moses, allowing the Scripture to shape our hearts before we dive into our work. The Psalter guide included in this book provides a pattern for reading the Psalms for organizational life. Reading the same Psalms together throughout the day creates a unified community of believers.

Some days, I hear the same Psalm as many as four or five times before lunch, and then another Psalm takes the stage for the afternoon. It is a simple rhythm that builds community, as we are all sharing in the same passages. No one has to prepare or study. We simply lean into this ancient way and walk in it.

It's Not About Us

I want to be careful here and repeat that I cannot claim this practice will create better outcomes for an organization. It may not lead to better performance or more revenue. This practice is aimed at one thing only: breathing God's Word out into the world as prayer.

The pattern of the world wants us to engage in practices that produce results and create an outcome in people. Strangely, I am suggesting this practice as something that can and should be done *irrespective of any measurable benefit*. Much like stopping at that scenic pullout on the highway, we may enjoy the view, and even rightly praise God for the beauty of his creation, but nothing material has been produced by our momentary diversion. Basking in the glory of God's creation can be work enough.

We must resist the urge to measure something that exists outside of the material realm. We live in an upside-down kingdom. God is willing to leave the ninety-nine and go in search of the one, and those metrics do not scale well from the perspective of the world's economy. This is a tension that Christian organizations live in. I think we must ensure that there is, in fact, this tension. We likely have drifted too far from a healthy space if we feel no tension at all.

So many times, we miss the point. In *Walden,* Henry David Thoreau writes of his fellow citizens' interest in fishing: "Commonly, they did not think that they were lucky or well paid for their time unless they got a long string of fish, *though they had the opportunity of seeing the pond all the while.*"[21] The pond, of course, is enough. Its simple existence is a precious thing.

So it is to read and pray the Psalms. Like a beautiful pond that is innately worth savoring regardless of how many fish bite that day, the Psalms have value simply in that they come from God and are his voice as verse and prayer. If we go to the Psalms or any Scripture and expect to receive personal gain like a string of fish, we will miss the opportunity to just *see* the pond.

The essence of this practice is simple: *theopneustos.* Breathe God's Word, the Psalms, out into the world again as prayer.

Summary—The Way of Interruption—Psalms

How to pray the Psalms as a team:

> 1. Engage in the practice of pausing,
> as described in the prior chapter.

> 2. Turn to the Psalm selected for the day
> in this book's included Psalter guide.

> 3. Read the Psalm as a prayer.

PRAY

"I take my little psalter, hurry to my room ... I say
the Ten Commandments, the Creed, and, if I have
time, some words of Christ or of Paul, or some Psalms,
out loud to myself just as a child might do."
—Martin Luther[22]

Collision of Prayer

Martin Luther wrote *A Simple Way to Pray* eighteen years after nailing
his Ninety-Five Theses to the church door at Wittenberg. He wrote
the little book for his barber, who had inquired on how he might
improve his prayer life. Luther leans into the ancient practice we
described previously: reading Scripture aloud, especially the Psalms.

Our concern here is with how the call to prayer collides with the
life of a parachurch ministry.

Organizational Prayer

What is the role of prayer in an organization? There are hundreds (if not thousands) of books on the prayer life of the individual, prayer in the life of the Church, and prayer in communities of vocational ministry. In their recent book, *Lead with Prayer*, Peter Greer and his coauthors begin to describe what prayer can look like in the life of a leader, and the last third of the book explores ways a leader may chart a course for prayer in their organization. It is a helpful resource that I commend to any reader. But even this book, one of the few I am aware of that even begins to touch on prayer in the life of an organization, does not get us to an answer to the question I posed above.

The fact is, in the life of the early Church, the Church and its work in the world were one. There were no parachurch ministries or Christian organizations apart from the Church for hundreds and hundreds of years. Since neither the apostles nor the early Church fathers contemplated this modern invention, we are left to look to Scripture for analogs of our present experience.

The apostle Paul was engaged in building the Church, and his work was inseparable from it. Paul was running a "church-planting" organization, if you will. I suggest that we can look at the requests Paul made for prayer and learn something that can help us find at least one way to answer the question of the role of prayer in the life of the organization.

Lord, Teach Us to Pray: Daily Bread and Kingdom Come

Paul repeatedly asked for the prayers of others in his letters to the various churches. His requests are quite similar in nature. In 2 Thessalonians 3:1, Ephesians 6:19, and Colossians 4:2–4, Paul asks for prayer for himself that he might "proclaim the word, the mystery of Christ." Colossians 4:3–4 says, "Pray for us, too, that God will give us many opportunities to speak about his mysterious plan concerning Christ. That is why I am here in chains. Pray that I will proclaim this message as clearly as I should."

Paul is inviting these churches to pray for his work, the work of spreading the word of the mystery of the gospel of Christ. This is Paul's main objective as an apostle. He almost never asks for prayer for personal issues or concerns, and when he does, they are for things that would prevent this main mission from being accomplished.

As the leader of a parachurch ministry, I believe this reveals a principle about prayer in organizational life: When you pray together, pray for things that are mission central and mission critical.

There are times and places for prayer for individual needs and concerns. We, "the Church"—by which I mean all believers—are called to pray for one another, to carry one another's burdens, to be the body of Christ. A Christian organization, on the other hand, is situated differently. It exists to achieve some aim or mission ordained by God to support his Church.

Organizational prayer can have a specific rhythm that emulates Paul's request of the churches. We should meet together to pray for our mission, our plans, our strategies, and their success. Success is, in my view, the degree to which the mystery of the gospel is made real in the world for others to see.

If you live in a Western church culture, you are aware that much of prayer is petitionary prayer for health, for well-being, for needs. The prayer Jesus taught us to pray certainly includes a request for God to provide "our daily bread." However, the first part of that timeless prayer has to do with God's will and his kingdom coming. This is the work of the Church, and the work of organizations that support the Church.

Over the last few years I have added the Lord's Prayer back into my daily personal practice. In this prayer that Jesus taught us, I have found a renewed sense of alignment with the Christ who taught these words and solace in knowing that these are the words he spoke.

Prayer in the life of the organization can take notes from Paul and from the Lord's Prayer. Above all other concerns, the focus of our prayers can be for God's kingdom to come on earth. Like Paul, we know God's kingdom comes as the mystery of the gospel of Christ is revealed in the hearts of men, women, and children.

Here is an example of a prayer I pray quite often in some way before a meeting:

"Lord, we invite you to empower us by your spirit to do your work in the world. You have called us to this mission and purpose. We need your assistance and mercy in following you in this task. We pray that as we go about this work, you will shape and conform us to the image of your Son. We pray also that as we pursue our mission, others would come to know the One in whose name we do this work and in whose name we pray. Amen."

Keeping It Simple

The Psalms are prayers. From Athanasius to Augustine, from Calvin to Merton, we are surrounded by a cloud of witnesses who all attest to the Psalms being prayers. In the West, it is not uncommon for many of us to feel a compulsion to add some of our own words or prayers after reading a perfectly good Psalm. If we can take a cue from our practice of pausing and take a moment after we read a Psalm to let it sink in, we may discover that no additional words are needed.

Psalm 51 calls to the depths of our being, bringing forth our brokenness and seeking God's grace and mercy. I have read this Psalm hundreds of times like many of you who are reading this. In almost every case I have found that the words of David are my words, and I need say no more. A simple "Amen, let it be so" is enough.

However, I also find that if we do choose to enter into spontaneous prayer on the heels of a reorienting pause and the timeworn words of the Psalms, it is easier to form our own words of praise and petition from a place of awe and awareness. I do two things in following this path:

1. I reach into the Psalm for a word, phrase, or image that sticks out, and center my prayer upon it. The hope is that this particular idea may, as Henri Nouwen says, "slowly build a little nest in our heart and stay there for the rest of our busy day."[23]
2. I invite the Holy Spirit to shape and conform us into the image of the Father and the Son so that our work will be shaped likewise.

Praying Together

I was talking to the CEO of an international ministry recently. He expressed his angst for many on his team when events arose, and they felt an obvious call to prayer but did not have the words. He wished he could provide them with a tool and resource that would remove the barrier that a global team sometimes has in accessing prayer together across languages and cultures.

Prayers as liturgy are a perfect bridge across this gap. Many churches use written prayer and liturgy as the heart of their services, and recent books like *Every Moment Holy* from Rabbit Room Press have tapped into the desire of people across the world who crave words to pray, privately and communally.

In our organization we have used shared prayers as a way to mark significant events in our organization and in the lives of team members. The last portion of this book provides you with an array of such prayers as liturgy, designed to mark many of these moments in the life of an organization. Use them to lean into the way of interruption.

Knowing that I am praying these words with other people in other organizations makes my heart swell with hope and faith.

My aim is to inspire you as a leader toward creating communal practices in your organization that bring God into the world and enable him to conform teams to his pattern in a mysterious way. *After all, shaping and conforming is not our work, it is his.*

Summary—The Way of Interruption—Pray

How to pray as a team:

1. Choose a word, image, or phrase from the day's Psalm; build your prayer around it, letting it build a nest in your heart and spill out into your work.

2. Ask God to shape your work.

3. Pray for your work, that it might be a part of God's kingdom come.

mountain

THE SIGH (AND A SUMMARY)

AS I WRITE about the way of interruption—pausing, reading the Psalms, and praying—I feel a deep sigh leaving my chest. It's like when, after one of those long days of work, you fall into your favorite chair and let out a long breath. That is how I feel every time we interrupt a busy day with these three simple practices. The way of interruption is these three things: slowing down through pausing, bringing the Spirit of God into the world as we breathe out Psalms together, and speaking prayers aimed at God shaping our mission. Now, whatever follows—whether it is a full agenda or a simple task—it can be met with this feeling of release. If you build these practices into your organizational life, you too will discover the power of this deep sigh and a whole new way of being. God is at work in our world in ways we cannot fully discern or appreciate. When we orient our teams to the divine in the world, we open a doorway for something of God to spill out into our world through the wardrobe. It is all a bit mysterious, but I like it that way.

Thomas R. Kelly writes in his book, *A Testament of Devotion*, "A practicing Christian must above all be one who practices the perpetual return of the soul into the inner sanctuary, who brings the world into its Light and rejudges it, who brings the Light into the world with all its turmoil and its fitfulness and recreates it."[24] My aim here is to call us to simple, consistent practices, practices that incorporate this idea of a perpetual return of our souls to God during the workday of Christian organizational life.

It is my belief that leaders in organizations have a dual burden: leading the effectiveness of the ministry or Christian enterprise while also trying to understand their role in shaping the spiritual life of the organization. Practices like those outlined here are simple steps to lead into the future by leaning into the past. G. K. Chesterton, in his book *Orthodoxy*, wrote, "I freely confess all the idiocy of *having all the* ambitions of the end of the nineteenth century. I did, like all other solemn little boys, try to be in advance of the age. Like them I tried to be some ten minutes in advance of the truth. And I found that I was eighteen hundred years behind it!"[25] With Chesterton, we find that the best new thing to discover is that wise people in the Church have already trod this path.

Lean into these simple practices. They are presented as a guide. Build or improve upon them if you will. If thinking about having every meeting begin this way seems like too high a bar, then develop your own way to pause, read a Psalm, and pray. Begin the day or end the day with Psalms and silence in your place of work.

The Way of Interruption is just one way, but it is a path to consider. If any part of this resource is useful to you and your organization, may God bless it. You may only use the prayers and liturgies—great. Perhaps the Psalter guide is something you want to use for just a season—fantastic. This book has been my attempt to draw your eyes to practices that might enable God to shape your organization regardless of your present practice or absence thereof.

I hope that many organizations will take these simple steps toward spiritual practice. Try it for thirty or sixty days. Run your own test.

What might God do if all across the world, we prayed together through the Psalms every day? I don't know, but I would love to find out!

To Sum Up—The Way of Interruption

Here's how to practice The Way of Interruption:

1. Pause:
    -   Remove distractions.
    -   Breathe—deeply, slowly, and silently (for thirty seconds to three minutes).
    -   While you pause and breathe, take every thought captive.
    -   While you pause and breathe, recollect yourself.

2. Psalms:
    -   Turn to the Psalm selected for the day in this book's included Psalter guide.
    -   Read the Psalm together as a prayer.

3. Pray:
    -   If you feel led to pray in your own words, choose a word, image, or phrase from the day's Psalm; build your prayer around it, letting it nest in your heart and spill out into your work.
    -   Ask God to shape your work and pray for that work that it might be a part of God's kingdom come.

ANNUAL PSALTER GUIDE

ALIGNING TO GOD'S AGENDA

JOHN CALVIN CALLED the Psalms "An Anatomy of all the Parts of the Soul." In the preface to his commentary on the Psalms, he goes on to say,

> "There is not an emotion of which anyone can be conscious that is not here represented as in a mirror. Or rather, the Holy Spirit has here drawn to the life all the griefs, sorrows, fears, doubts, hopes, cares, perplexities, in short, all the distracting emotions with which the minds of men are wont to be agitated. ... There is no other book in which there are to be found more express and magnificent commendations, both of the unparalleled liberality of God towards his Church and of all his works; there is no other book in which there is recorded so many deliverances nor one in which the evidence and experiences of the fatherly providence and concern which God exercises towards us are celebrated with such splendor of diction, and yet with the strictest adherence

to truth; in short, there is no other book in which we are more perfectly taught the right manner of praising God, or in which we are more powerfully stirred up to the performance of this religious exercise."[26]

The Psalms can serve as the anchor and rallying point for organizations. Calvin certainly makes the case for their use in all areas of life, and here, we find their intersection with organizational rhythms.

There are hundreds of reading plans for the Psalms, but I have yet to find any directed toward a work rhythm. The following section of the book is our solution to this gap. We have laid out the first week of Psalms (using the New Living Translation) to help you visualize the plan. Following this is the cycle for reading the Psalms as an organization. We also have a link and a QR code that gives you and your team free access to the full calendar of readings for each year as a PDF, or you can receive them each day in your inbox. Using a five-day work week, teams will read through all the Psalms every 130 workdays, twice a year.

There are times when the Psalm for the day, by being broken into parts, will leave a tension in the air. This may feel uncomfortable to sit in the lament without the resolution of the Psalm closing. I have found this a welcome change that permits parts of Psalms to cause reflection or even a sort of shock to the system. There are other times when, to maintain connection to the Psalm, a verse at the beginning will be repeated from the previous reading.

Interrupting your work to become present and to speak a Psalm together will shape and conform the work you do and reorient the moment to God and his agenda. You will be joining other organizations and leaders in reading the same Psalm each morning and afternoon, raising our collective voices with others to God. This is the invitation I hope you will accept.

Paraphrasing Thomas R. Kelly in his book *A Testament of Devotion*, what is here urged are internal practices aimed at orienting the depths of our being so that our internal life is perpetually bowed in worship.[27] Is there any higher aim for us in our work? What might the work and mission of your organization look like if you, your staff, your team, and your partners all lived lives perpetually bowed in worship?

THE PLAN: WEEK 1

Monday Morning

Psalm 1

1   Oh, the joys of those who do not
    follow the advice of the wicked,
    or stand around with sinners,
    or join in with mockers.
2   But they delight in the law of the LORD, meditating on it day and night.
3   They are like trees planted along the riverbank,
    bearing fruit each season.
    Their leaves never wither,
    and they prosper in all they do.
4   But not the wicked!
    They are like worthless chaff, scattered by the wind.
5   They will be condemned at the time of judgment.
    Sinners will have no place among the godly.
6   For the LORD watches over the path of the godly,
    but the path of the wicked leads to destruction.

Monday Afternoon

Psalm 2

1 Why are the nations so angry?
Why do they waste their time with futile plans?
2 The kings of the earth prepare for battle;
the rulers plot together
against the LORD
and against his anointed one.
3 "Let us break their chains," they cry,
"and free ourselves from slavery to God."
4 But the one who rules in heaven laughs.
The Lord scoffs at them.
5 Then in anger he rebukes them,
terrifying them with his fierce fury.
6 For the Lord declares, "I have placed my chosen king on the throne
in Jerusalem, on my holy mountain."
7 The king proclaims the LORD's decree:
"The LORD said to me, 'You are my son.
Today I have become your Father.
8 Only ask, and I will give you the nations as your inheritance,
the whole earth as your possession.
9 You will break them with an iron rod
and smash them like clay pots.'"
10 Now then, you kings, act wisely!
Be warned, you rulers of the earth!
11 Serve the LORD with reverent fear,
and rejoice with trembling.
12 Submit to God's royal son, or he will become angry,
and you will be destroyed in the midst of all your activities—
for his anger flares up in an instant.
But what joy for all who take refuge in him!

Tuesday Morning

Psalm 3

1 O LORD, I have so many enemies;
    so many are against me.
2 So many are saying,
    "God will never rescue him!"
3 But you, O LORD, are a shield around me;
    you are my glory, the one who holds my head high.
4 I cried out to the LORD,
    and he answered me from his holy mountain.
5 I lay down and slept,
    yet I woke up in safety,
    for the LORD was watching over me.
6 I am not afraid of ten thousand enemies
    who surround me on every side.
7 Arise, O LORD!
    Rescue me, my God!
    Slap all my enemies in the face!
    Shatter the teeth of the wicked!
8 Victory comes from you, O LORD.
    May you bless your people.

Tuesday Afternoon

Psalm 4

1   Answer me when I call to you,
    O God who declares me innocent.
    Free me from my troubles.
    Have mercy on me and hear my prayer.
2   How long will you people ruin my reputation?
    How long will you make groundless accusations?
    How long will you continue your lies?
3   You can be sure of this:
    The LORD set apart the godly for himself.
    The LORD will answer when I call to him.
4   Don't sin by letting anger control you.
    Think about it overnight and remain silent.
5   Offer sacrifices in the right spirit,
    and trust the LORD.
6   Many people say, "Who will show us better times?"
    Let your face smile on us, LORD.
7   You have given me greater joy
    than those who have abundant harvests of grain and new wine.
8   In peace I will lie down and sleep,
    for you alone, O LORD, will keep me safe.

Wednesday Morning

Psalm 5

1   O LORD, hear me as I pray;
     pay attention to my groaning.

2   Listen to my cry for help, my King and my God,
     for I pray to no one but you.

3   Listen to my voice in the morning, LORD.
     Each morning I bring my requests to you and wait expectantly.

4   O God, you take no pleasure in wickedness;
     you cannot tolerate the sins of the wicked.

5   Therefore, the proud may not stand in your presence,
     for you hate all who do evil.

6   You will destroy those who tell lies.
     The LORD detests murderers and deceivers.

7   Because of your unfailing love, I can enter your house;
     I will worship at your Temple with deepest awe.

8   Lead me in the right path, O LORD,
     or my enemies will conquer me.
     Make your way plain for me to follow.

9   My enemies cannot speak a truthful word.
     Their deepest desire is to destroy others.
     Their talk is foul, like the stench from an open grave.
     Their tongues are filled with flattery.

10 O God, declare them guilty.
     Let them be caught in their own traps.
     Drive them away because of their many sins,
     for they have rebelled against you.

11 But let all who take refuge in you rejoice;
     let them sing joyful praises forever.
     Spread your protection over them,
     that all who love your name may be filled with joy.

12 For you bless the godly, O LORD;
     you surround them with your shield of love.

Wednesday Afternoon

Psalm 6

1   O LORD, don't rebuke me in your anger
    or discipline me in your rage.
2   Have compassion on me, LORD, for I am weak.
    Heal me, LORD, for my bones are in agony.
3   I am sick at heart.
    How long, O LORD, until you restore me?
4   Return, O LORD, and rescue me.
    Save me because of your unfailing love.
5   For the dead do not remember you.
    Who can praise you from the grave?
6   I am worn out from sobbing.
    All night I flood my bed with weeping,
    drenching it with my tears.
7   My vision is blurred by grief;
    my eyes are worn out because of all my enemies.
8   Go away, all you who do evil,
    for the LORD has heard my weeping.
9   The LORD has heard my plea;
    the LORD will answer my prayer.
10   May all my enemies be disgraced and terrified.
    May they suddenly turn back in shame.

Thursday Morning

Psalm 7:1–9

1   I come to you for protection, O LORD my God.
Save me from my persecutors—rescue me!
2   If you don't, they will maul me like a lion,
tearing me to pieces with no one to rescue me.
3   O LORD my God, if I have done wrong
or am guilty of injustice,
4   if I have betrayed a friend
or plundered my enemy without cause,
5   then let my enemies capture me.
Let them trample me into the ground
and drag my honor in the dust.
6   Arise, O LORD, in anger!
Stand up against the fury of my enemies!
Wake up, my God, and bring justice!
7   Gather the nations before you.
Rule over them from on high.
8   The LORD judges the nations.
Declare me righteous, O LORD,
for I am innocent, O Most High!
9   End the evil of those who are wicked,
and defend the righteous.
For you look deep within the mind and heart,
O righteous God.

Thursday Afternoon

Psalm 7:10–17

10 God is my shield,
    saving those whose hearts are true and right.
11 God is an honest judge.
    He is angry with the wicked every day.
12 If a person does not repent,
    God will sharpen his sword;
    he will bend and string his bow.
13 He will prepare his deadly weapons
    and shoot his flaming arrows.
14 The wicked conceive evil;
    they are pregnant with trouble
    and give birth to lies.
15 They dig a deep pit to trap others,
    then fall into it themselves.
16 The trouble they make for others backfires on them.
    The violence they plan falls on their own heads.
17 I will thank the LORD because he is just;
    I will sing praise to the name of the LORD Most High.

Friday Morning

Psalm 8

1 O LORD, our Lord, your majestic name fills the earth!
   Your glory is higher than the heavens.
2 You have taught children and infants
   to tell of your strength,
   silencing your enemies
   and all who oppose you.
3 When I look at the night sky and see the work of your fingers—
   the moon and the stars you set in place—
4 what are mere mortals that you should think about them,
   human beings that you should care for them?
5 Yet you made them only a little lower than God
   and crowned them with glory and honor.
6 You gave them charge of everything you made,
   putting all things under their authority—
7 the flocks and the herds
   and all the wild animals,
8 the birds in the sky, the fish in the sea,
   and everything that swims the ocean currents.
9 O LORD, our Lord, your majestic name fills the earth!

Friday Afternoon

Psalm 9:1–12

1   I will praise you, LORD, with all my heart;
    I will tell of all the marvelous things you have done.
2   I will be filled with joy because of you.
    I will sing praises to your name, O Most High.
3   My enemies retreated;
    they staggered and died when you appeared.
4   For you have judged in my favor;
    from your throne you have judged with fairness.
5   You have rebuked the nations and destroyed the wicked;
    you have erased their names forever.
6   The enemy is finished, in endless ruins;
    the cities you uprooted are now forgotten.
7   But the LORD reigns forever,
    executing judgment from his throne.
8   He will judge the world with justice
    and rule the nations with fairness.
9   The LORD is a shelter for the oppressed,
    a refuge in times of trouble.
10 Those who know your name trust in you,
    for you, O LORD, do not abandon those who search for you.
11 Sing praises to the LORD who reigns in Jerusalem.
    Tell the world about his unforgettable deeds.
12 For he who avenges murder cares for the helpless.
    He does not ignore the cries of those who suffer.

ACCESS TO THE ANNUAL PSALTER GUIDE

Download a PDF of the annual Psalter guide by going to www.billsimmons.net or by scanning this QR code:

You can also enter your email address and receive the Psalms daily in your inbox.

Join other organizations in reading in the same rhythm and let's see what God might do among us and through us.

PRAYERS AND LITURGIES

SHAPING OUR LIVES TOGETHER

"LITURGY" AND "LITURGICAL" were words that seemed archaic and stiff to me for much of my adult Christian life. Rote, pre-determined prayers, recited as a group? How stifling. It's not clear to me if that fiercely independent response is something inherited from American culture or from my human nature. Whatever the cause, it took God many years to draw me into a desire to participate with others in the work and action of shared prayer and devotion.

The word liturgy is often defined as a "work of the people" or "public service" from the Greek root. But I wanted to be me, not a part of "the people." I wanted to pray "my way" and on "my terms." In our modern culture, we are surrounded by a kaleidoscope of ways and means to pray and assured of our right to choose to worship however works best for us. But in the life of an organization, we are tasked with reflecting on how to reconcile our personal perspectives, the perspectives and cultures of our teams, and the long-standing traditions of the Church.

The disciples had been with Jesus for a few years when they finally asked him to teach them how to pray. We may suppose that Jesus likely did not use the Lord's Prayer himself whenever he went away to pray. Presumably, his life of communion and being one with the Father often extended beyond the usefulness of words. But, when pressed for a pattern they might imitate, he gave the disciples a clear path and words to follow.

The Lord's Prayer, the Our Father, is now used so often that perhaps some think it is worn out. "Why would I pray the Lord's Prayer? Sports teams pray this with no heart all the time. It has lost its relevance," some may say. I beg to differ. How can any of the words of Christ become stale or irrelevant? He who was and is the Word, the *logos* made flesh, spoke many things, and we can hold onto them as right and true all these years later.

What can be more precious than praying, alone or with others, the words our savior taught us to pray? Jesus gave no preface to this prayer other than, "Pray like this." The early Church adopted this prayer and has been practicing it ever since. Similarly, the Church fathers and others began to add to this other shared prayers; many times, these flowed out of the prophets, poetic passages, and the Psalms. These prayers and liturgies became practices and have been the shared work of Christians for thousands of years.

Many Protestants are accustomed to praying the Lord's Prayer. In almost all uses of the prayer, there is an addition not found in the oldest manuscripts nor in almost all modern translations. In Matthew 6:13 and Luke 11:4, the Lord's Prayer ends simply with, "Deliver us from evil." Yet most of us cannot help but end the prayer with, "For thine is the kingdom, the power, and the glory, forever and ever. Amen." This is considered the doxology[28] to the Lord's Prayer.

An ancient document called the Didache, which is dated from the late first century to the mid-second century, is the first recorded use of the doxology. The doxology was added to the 1611 King James Version, since it was an accepted practice by that time in the Church.

The point is that the Church found ways to share in prayer together from the very beginning, and the liturgy grew along with the living out of the words of the Gospels and the apostles. From the doxology to the sacrament of baptism, whether the teachings of the Reformed, Roman Catholic, or Orthodox, we all share practices whose origins stem from the contributions of both the apostles as well as the early Church fathers.

Christians have used psalms, creeds, and liturgy to shape their lives for millennia. The liturgical prayers included on the ensuing pages are prayers that may be used together or privately for moments that arise in the life of an organization. The act of praying in one voice with others (whether metaphorically or in a literal chorus) brings us together in the unity of the spirit as the Church. This was Jesus's prayer in the Gospel of John, that we would be one as he and the Father are one.[29] Liturgies and prayers are a visible sign of our unity with each other and with God.

When we use these in our organization, our team may introduce the liturgy with sayings or a Scripture that fits the person or the local context. Then we use the liturgy as provided, thus striking a balance between uniformity and flexibility.

These prayers and liturgies have been designed to assist in the moments that arise in an organization. Many executives and leaders, myself included, crafted the prayers at the heart of these liturgies. May these be a resource to you as you lead your organization through critical moments in enlarging God's kingdom on earth.

The liturgical prayers included can be prayed by a group in one voice, read by one leader on behalf of the group, or used as a call and response, with the leader taking the italicized sections and the group joining together for the pieces that remain. You may also find they are a great resource for private prayer for these same events.

It is my prayer that many people and organizations might together use these prayers. In so doing, through our shared voices, may God in his mercy hear our prayers.

LITURGIES FOR EVERYDAY NEEDS AND TASKS

To Celebrate God's Provision

O God, our cup overflows![30]

We praise you, Lord, with all our hearts;
We will tell of the marvelous things you have done.
We are filled with joy because of you.
We sing praises to your name, O Most High.[31]

Lord, we come before you and humbly thank you for continuing to provide
for our needs. You never cease to surprise us.

In our daily bread
and your kingdom come
and our deliverance from evil.[32]
In the little things and the moving of mountains.
In the feeding of sparrows and the adorning of flowers.[33]
You shepherd us well, O God.
We have all that we need.
Green meadows and peaceful streams,
strength renewed along right paths.
Surely, your goodness and unfailing love will pursue us
all of our days.[34]

Everything we are and everything we have is from you, O Lord.

You provide for us daily, and daily, we praise your name.

Amen.

Created in collaboration with Pamela Armstrong-Pautz, Hope Rises International

To Request God's Provision

The Lord is our shepherd; we shall not want.[35]

The eyes of all look to you in hope;
you give us all we need.
When you open your hand,
you satisfy the hunger and thirst of every living thing.
You are righteous and full of kindness;
you are close to all who call upon you in truth.[36]

Father God, you are Jehovah Jireh: the Lord that provides. We come before you with humble hearts, acknowledging our dependence on your abundant grace. Your Word assures us that you are our Provider, and we trust in your promise to meet all our needs. As we face uncertainty and struggle, we plead for your provision, confident that you will supply according to your riches in glory.

We were born weak and defenseless, but from the cradle, you have defended us.
All our lives, you have wondrously guided us, your love illuminating the path;
all who call upon your name give thanks, for you always provide.[37]

We thank you for your faithfulness and for the blessings you are preparing for us. Help us to remain steadfast in faith, knowing that you are always with us, guiding and sustaining us.

Christ, have mercy upon us.

Amen.

Created in collaboration with Pamela Armstrong-Pautz, Hope Rises International

For Discernment

O God, we cry out for your guidance.

We tune our ears to wisdom,
and concentrate on understanding.
We beg for insight.
We search for these things as for silver and seek them like hidden treasures.
For we know that you grant wisdom,
knowledge, understanding,
and a treasure of common sense to the honest.[38]

Lord, as we discuss and deliberate, lead us to discern your will. We
humbly submit to your Holy Spirit and ask that you prompt, guide, and
direct us. Let our human reasoning and imagining reflect your will and
purpose in our lives.

Lord, let it be so.

We pray that individually and corporately we will be attuned and respon-
sive to how your spirit is leading. Give us the courage to express openly
what we hear you say and the commitment to act in obedience.

Though our minds are like brief syllables
compared to the pureness of sound that you are,
O great I AM,
we know that you can stretch us as wide as the sky
and deep as the sea
to begin to contain the understanding and wisdom we need today.[39]

Lord, hear our prayer.

Amen.

Created in collaboration with Ken Wilson, Hope Rises International

For an Audit

Lord, everything that is good comes from you.

We sing out our thanks
for the rain and the grass,
for your provision of all we have.
You feed even the young ravens when they cry,
and take no pleasure in human might.
No, you delight in those who hope in your unfailing love.
And God, we hope in you.[40]

You have entrusted us with many gifts, and we seek to steward them wisely all the year long. We ask you to help us to stand humbly and firmly in the face of scrutiny. Make our memories sound and our spirits calm.

We commit our actions to you.[41]
God, establish the work of our hands.[42]

For how beautiful on the mountains
are the feet of the messenger who brings good news,
the good news of peace and salvation,
the news that the God of Israel reigns![43]

Lord, have mercy on us. Christ, have mercy on us.

Wrap us in your peace as we answer for the work that we have done, that
we may continue to do that good work.

Amen.

Created in collaboration with Beverly Elmore, Hope Rises International

For Travel

O Lord, you are with us in our comings and goings.

Through deep waters,
through rivers of difficulty,
through the fire,
you are with us wherever we go.[44]

Heavenly Father, as (Name) starts this journey, we place our trust in you.
Thank you for the ability to travel, that we may visit cities and countries
to engage in the work you have called us to. May we carry the message of
Christ with us as we go.

Christ, be with us and be with (Name) as he/she travels.
Christ before us and behind us,
in us, beneath us, and above us,
on our right and on our left,
when we lie down, sit, and arise.[45]
God, we ask for safe travels and smooth logistics. We pray (Name) arrives
refreshed and of clear mind, ready to serve you.

Lord, be with us all.

Amen.

Created in collaboration with Melissa Edmiston, Hope Rises International

For Research

O Lord, light a path for our feet.

For we know and attest
that we have received gifts from you
to steward your grace in its many forms
and to serve others well.[46]

Sovereign God, in love, you created us in your image and have set us in this time and place as your ambassadors.
You have given each of us gifts to serve others as stewards of your grace. Grant us hearts of curiosity to see what we currently do not see and humility to receive it with gratitude.

Open our eyes, O Lord.

Guide us in this research, from design to dissemination, to discover new opportunities to impact and benefit those we serve. We pray for your spirit of integrity to conduct this research with transparency and love for all. Jesus, help us to lay aside our egos to open a space for honoring differences in perspectives with wisdom rooted in your truth.

Let this research draw people closer to you.
May it help us be better stewards and managers of the gifts you have given us.

In your grace, bless and guide each of us to know your design for loving you and others in all circumstances.

Glory to the Father, and to the Son, and to the Holy Spirit.

Amen.

Created in collaboration with Jason Paltzer, Meros Center

.

For the Healing of a Coworker

Jesus, Son of David, have mercy. Father of all, have mercy. Christ our Lord, have mercy.

We praise your holy name and never forget your goodness:
you forgive our sins
heal our diseases,
redeem us from death,
crown us with love,
and renew our youth like the eagle's.[47]

Lord of all creation, who shows compassion and mercy to us, his creatures, we pray for healing for (Name). Please sustain him/her by your power, giving him/her your mighty strength. Father God, you establish our steps and lift up those who are weighed down. May (Name) trust in you and experience your unfailing love day by day.

We pray that your peace will flood (Name's) heart and mind as you work out your will in his/her life.

Now to him who is able to do immeasurably more than all we ask or imagine, according to his power that is at work within us, to him be glory in the Church and in Christ Jesus throughout all generations, forever and ever![48]

Amen.

Created in collaboration with Sarah Hesshaus, Hope Rises International

LITURGIES FOR BEGINNINGS
AND ENDINGS

For the Launch of a New Microenterprise

O God, open our eyes.

We give thanks to the Lord, for he is good!
There is joy for those who deal justly with others
and strive to do what is right.[49]
May the goodness of God drive us forward.

Lord, may your love move us from complacency to action.

As we begin new microenterprise programs and expand into new places
of service, help us see beyond just the needs—and notice the creativity,
gifts, and capacity in those we will serve.

Lord, open our eyes.

Allow us to listen to you and to those we serve.

Lord, open our ears.

And help this not be about a program or an organization but rather a
picture of the global Church in action.

Lord, open our hearts.

O God, break our hearts open
to the world
that we may never cease in love and action.

We commit this work to you, asking that it would help people see and
hear you, Jesus.

Amen.

Created in collaboration with Peter Greer, HOPE International

For the Launch of a New Strategy

God, you make all things new.

You are doing a new thing.
It springs up,
a way in the wilderness,
streams in the desert.[50]
Guide us as we do our own small new thing
for your glory.

*Lord, we commit this strategy to you. Take the work we have done together
and through discernment, following your spirit's lead, grant us success
through its implementation. May our work and diligence be a reflection
of your glory and a testament to your provision.*

Lord, through all the generations
you have been our home!
Before the mountains were born,
before you gave birth to the earth and the world,
from beginning to end, you are God.
Let us, your servants, see you work again;
let our children see your glory.
And may the Lord our God show us his approval
and make our efforts successful.
Yes, make our efforts successful![51]

*We pray that this strategy will be an instrument of good, and that it
will multiply blessings to families, communities, and nations. Let us also
remain sensitive to your spirit, holding our own plans loosely, remaining
open to your guidance, knowing your ways and will are better and higher
than ours.*

Our overarching strategy is to be in the center of your will—to use the gifts, abilities, and resources entrusted to us to remain there. This we pray.

O Lord, hear our prayer.

Amen.

Created in collaboration with Ken Wilson, Hope Rises International

For the Launch of a New Project

God, bless the work of our hands.

Unless the Lord builds a house,
the work of the builders is wasted.[52]
Lord, we long to join with you in your work.
Establish our steps today.

Heavenly Father, as we launch this new project, we ask for your guidance and blessing. Thank you for the provision of resources that allow us to begin (project). Grant us wisdom in our decisions, grace in our collaboration, and favor in our implementation.

God, the pitcher cries for water to carry
and a person for work that is real.[53]
Let us do this good and real work well.
Let us love our neighbors well.
Lord, let it be so.

May this project be a reflection of your love and facilitate healing and renewed hope.

Lord, hear our prayer.

Amen.

Created in collaboration with Melissa Edmiston, Hope Rises International

For the Launch of a New Business Venture

Lord, it was you who commanded us to be fruitful and multiply[54] after declaring, "It was good."[55] May this venture multiply your good, O Lord.

Lord, you know we are not like you, who merely spoke,
and the heavens were created;
Simply breathed the word,
and all the stars were born.
We stand in awe of you!
Be with us as we labor, too, to begin something new.[56]

Give your entrepreneur the wisdom to discern your will, give them the courage to follow your ways, and give them the strength to work for the good of all so that in all things, they may honor you. O Lord, bless the work of their hands and minds, that their efforts may be fruitful and pleasing in your sight.

Grant them the grace to use their talents wisely and for the good of others. Grant them, O Lord, the wisdom to understand your will, the prudence to act in accordance with it, and the strength to persevere in your service. Give life to this mustard seed, this business now sewn, and grow it large that good works, human dignity, and life might abound in its shade.[57]

Lord, hear our prayer.

Amen.

Created in collaboration with Peter Greer, HOPE International

For One Departing on Sabbatical

As (Name) goes into a season of ceasing, Lord, may his/her heart be set on pilgrimage. Look favorably on him/her, withhold no good thing from him/her, and may he/she enter a season of fully resting in the shadow of your wings.

May (Name's) soul truly find rest in God;
may he/she know that salvation comes from you.
Be his/her rock and salvation;
be a fortress for him/her, may he/she never be shaken.[58]

God of mercy, we come to you with one heart.
In this brief parting, may your mercy go with (Name).
We invite you to be the vinedresser in his/her life
as he/she enters a time of ceasing.
Christ, have mercy on us.
Bring our brother/sister your spiritual water,
That his/her life may overflow.
Christ, have mercy on us.
May he/she find your easy burden,
And true rest for his/her soul.
Christ, have mercy on us.
We commit him/her now to you and your merciful care,
May he/she lay her work down as he/she departs
And permit the soil of his/her life to lie fallow these coming months.

Christ, have mercy on us.

May (Name's) mind come to rest and be tended in ways that he/she cannot intend. May he/she be borne, preserved, and comprehended by what he/she cannot comprehend. May your sabbath, Lord, thus keep him/her by your will, not by his/hers.[59]

Lord, these are our prayers for (Name). We pray for all these blessings through our Lord Jesus Christ, your Son, who lives and reigns with you in the unity of the Holy Spirit, God, forever and ever.

Amen.

Created by the author

For One Returning from Sabbatical

God, we greet you and invite you, by your grace and mercy, to meet us as we receive among us one who has been away in your sabbath rest. We rejoice in his/her return.

We give you thanks
for sheltering him/her,
and for being his/her place of refuge in this time of sabbatical rest.

May the grace you have shown to (Name) be shown to us as he/she returns, and like Moses's face glowed[60] and the people could see he had been in your presence, may the glow of rest also reach us as (Name) returns to our midst.

Lord, in all our work, may we see the grace with which you sustain all things.

Lord, our shepherd, you restore our souls.

Lord, we are thankful for (Name) and his/her time away resting in you. Thank you for being his/her shepherd and for leading, guiding and refreshing him/her. In this return to work, may his/her walk with you encourage each of us to trust in you more as our shepherd.

Lord, our shepherd, you restore our souls.

May we be a support to (Name) as he/she reintegrates into our mission and work.
Lord, let the knowledge of salvation enlighten our hearts,
so that, freed from fear and from the power of our enemies,
we may serve you faithfully all the days of our life.

We ask for all of this through our Lord Jesus Christ, your Son,
who lives and reigns with you and the Holy Spirit,
God, for ever and ever.

Amen.

Created by the author

For Those Beginning Parental Leave

Father, we thank you for this gift: a bright, precious, and new life.

You made all the delicate, inner parts of this baby's body
and knit him/her together, oh so tenderly,
in the dark and quiet of the womb.
And every day of his/her life is already recorded in your book.
You know this child,
and you are with him/her, even now.[61]

*Father, God, we know that children are a gift from you.[62] Bless this baby
and his/her parents. Help them adjust to a new way of being as they
welcome this new little person into their hearts and home. Give them
strength when sleepless nights stretch long.*

O God, you gather your children as a mother hen protects her chicks
under her wings.[63]
You know what it is to love beyond what we can imagine.

*Love as warm as tears,
as fierce as fire,
as fresh as spring,
as hard as nails.[64]
Thank you for blessing this family with a shimmering shard of that love,
and be with them in their comings and goings.*

Father, God, may they feel your presence as they navigate the challenges and joys of parenthood. Cover their home in peace, grace, and love, and fill it with joy and laughter.

Amen.

Created in collaboration with Beverly Elmore, Hope Rises International

For One Who Is Transitioning Roles Internally

O God, go ahead of (Name). You will not fail or abandon him/her.[65]

May he/she trust in the Lord and do good.
Then he/she will live safely in the land and prosper.
May he/she take delight in the Lord,
committing every action
and trusting in God's help.[66]

Eternal Father in heaven, as our friend and teammate (Name) transitions to a new role, we trust you to guide him/her on the pathway of life.

For we know
our own ears will hear you.
Right behind us a voice will say,
"This is the way you should go,"
whether to the right or to the left.[67]

May all of us, along with those you prepare, exude friendship, goodwill, grace, and clarity to (Name).

Lord, have mercy.

May he/she pass the baton with wisdom, lessons on listening, and assertive graciousness.

Christ, have mercy.

May he/she receive the baton and run the next leg of this race with resolve, stamina, and tenacity.

Lord, these are our prayers for (Name).

We pray for all these blessings through our Lord Jesus Christ, your Son, who lives and reigns with you in the unity of the Holy Spirit, God, forever and ever.

Amen.

Created in collaboration with Jim Oehrig, Hope Rises International

For One Who Is Retiring

O God, we know that there is a time for everything.

A time to plant and a time to harvest.
A time to tear down and a time to build up.
A time to grieve and a time to dance.
A time to scatter stones and a time to gather stones.
A time to embrace and a time to turn away.
A time to search and a time to quit searching.
A time to keep and a time to throw away.
A time to tear and a time to mend.
A time to be quiet and a time to speak.[68]

Lord, as you have granted (Name) strength to work and contribute in his/her calling, so grant him/her peace of heart while entering this new phase of life. Give him/her grace, patience, and forbearance to finish well the task laid before him/her, and to guard the relationships entrusted to him/her through his/her work.

To be blessed is to live and work
so hard that God's love washes right through you.[69]
So has it been for (Name).
God, bless (Name), who has all our gratitude and all our love.
May he/she trust that you are leading his/her feet into a hopeful future.

God, grant (Name) an excitement and passion for what lies in store beyond full-time paid employment—a glimpse of life, ministry, and engagement at a different pace, with different people, groups, and activities, but still with you at the center of his/her being. Release him/her from any fear and uncertainty of the unknown and fill him/her with hope for whatever lies ahead.

Lord, we know there is a time for everything.

Christ, have mercy upon us and walk with us in the unknown.

Amen.

Created in collaboration with Ken Wilson, Hope Rises International

For When a Staff Member Leaves

Heavenly Father, you direct our steps and your plans are perfect.

(Name), may the Lord bless you
and protect you.
May the Lord smile on you
and be gracious to you.
May the Lord show you his favor
and give you his peace.[70]

God, we thank you for the time that we shared with (Name) and the blessing he/she has been to us and this organization. We ask for your blessing on him/her as he/she moves onto new adventures. We pray that you would fill the gap in our organization left by this departure, and that you would equip (Name) for what lies ahead.

We have stood with you shoulder to shoulder,
and now we let you go.
(Name), we send you off with love.

May the grace of the Lord Jesus Christ, and the love of God, and the fellowship of the Holy Spirit be with us all.[71]

Amen.

Created in collaboration with Sarah Hesshaus, Hope Rises International

For Welcoming a New Staff Member

O God, we rejoice today!

We exalt you, our God and King,
and praise your name forever and ever.
We will praise you every day;
yes, we will praise you forever.
Great is the Lord! He is most worthy of praise!
No one can measure his greatness.[72]

Lord God, thank you for bringing (Name) into our team. We thank you for (Name), the gifts you have given to him/her and for how you have prepared him/her for this role, at this time, and in this place. We ask that you integrate him/her into the team, helping him/her to learn and adapt. We pray that we would be welcoming and equip him/her for success.

Come, let us care for one another as God has cared for us!

We give you all the glory for bringing (Name) to our team and pray your blessing on him/her in the name of the Father, Son, and Holy Spirit.

Amen.

Created in collaboration with Sarah Hesshaus, Hope Rises International

For Welcoming a New Leader

God, we welcome (Name) as you have welcomed us into your family.

God, remind us:
Whoever wants to be a leader must become a servant,
For even the Son of Man came not to be served, but to serve.[73]

Mighty God, thank you for bringing (Name) to our team and our organization. Thank you for all the ways you have prepared him/her to serve you in this leadership role.

We pray for your blessing on (Name):
for wisdom and guidance, humility and grace, strength and peace.

May (Name) keep his/her eyes fixed on Jesus.

Please graft (Name) into this team.

Help him/her as he/she learns about the organization, the team, and the role.

We ask that you bless our shared mission and that we would be steadfast, immovable, always abounding in the work of the Lord, knowing that in the Lord our labor is not in vain.[74]

Amen.

Created in collaboration with Sarah Hesshaus, Hope Rises International

LITURGIES FOR GATHERINGS AND RELATIONSHIPS

For a Gathering of Donors

Guide our steps, O Lord.

The earth is the Lord's, and everything in it.
The world and all its people belong to him.
For he laid the earth's foundation on the seas
and built it on the ocean depths.[75]

Whatever we receive, O Lord, we bless your name.

We lift up our hearts to you God, asking for your guidance and blessing
as we gather donors to support your work in the world. We pray that you
move in the hearts of those called to contribute, inspiring them to give
generously and joyfully for the advancement of your kingdom. Lord, we
humbly ask that you surround us with kingdom partners who love you
and love people.

May our donors' contributions be used wisely to spread your love and
grace, to be your hands and feet, reaching those with the good news, and
may they see the impact of their gifts in transforming lives and expanding
your reach.

Bless this effort, Lord, and let it bring glory to your name.

Amen.

Created in collaboration with Pamela Armstrong-Pautz, Hope Rises International

For a Board Meeting

Lord, come to our assistance.

Help us begin this meeting by pouring your Holy Spirit into us so that we might be filled with wisdom for right decision-making. This mission, and this work you have called us to steward, needs your guidance.

God, as we discuss and decide,
let us be like David:
shepherding with integrity of heart
and skillful hands.[76]

May we keep your plans and vision ever before us, being more interested in where you want us to go than how staff helps us get there. Keep the people we serve ever before our hearts and minds. May we put aside our own plans and interests while in this space and embrace the needs of good governance and prayerful decisions.

This is your work; use us as your people to reach others in your name.

We ask all of this in the name of your Son, Jesus Christ, our Lord.

Amen.

Created by the author

For a Staff Gathering

God, be with us. We gather as one in your holy name.

How good it is
when brothers and sisters live together in harmony!
Harmony as precious as the anointing oil
that ran down Aaron's head, into his beard and his robe.
Harmony as refreshing as the dew on the mountains of Zion.[77]

May we encourage one another to craft and create; conceptualize and codesign; to collaborate and commemorate our plans, projects, and results.

Lord, let it be so.

May we lay aside our own agendas and petty preferences, yearning for your grace and mercy to abound as we implement and live out the fine print of your master plan.

Lord, let it be so.

May the outcomes and products of this gathering point to you and your eternal principles.

Lord, let it be so.

As we gather together,
Christ is in our midst.
He is and ever shall be.

Amen.

Created in collaboration with Jim Oehrig, Hope Rises International

For an Everyday Meeting

Lord, empower us by your spirit to do your work in the world.

Let us remember what that good work truly is,
what you require of us:
to do what is right, to love mercy,
and to walk humbly with you.[78]

You have called us to our mission and purpose. We need your assistance
in following you in today's task.

We are the clay,
and you are the potter.[79]
Mold us, O Lord.

We pray that you would shape and conform us to the image of your Son
as we go about this work. As we pursue our mission, may others come to
know the One in whose name we do this work and in whose name we pray.

Amen.

Created by the author

For Partnerships

O God, bless our partnerships—these cords of three strands.[80]

We are a body composed of many parts,
and all are different,
and all are one in you.
If one part suffers, all the parts suffer with it,
and if one part is honored, all the parts are glad.
Lord, let us come together in harmony.[81]

Holy Spirit, instill in us the drive and determination to establish, nurture, and protect the partners and partnerships you have granted to us. We recognize our earthly relationships are dependent on our vertical relationship with you.

As with Moses when he stood, arms uplifted,
supported on either side by Aaron and Hur,
let us keep our hands steady till sunset,[82]
leaning on one another as we pursue your kingdom on earth.
May the groups and organizations with whom we collaborate cultivate koinonia and connection, faith and friendship, and empathy and excellence as we customize our commitments to your people, your Word, and that which breaks your heart.

Lord, let it be so.

May we view each partner as coworkers entrusted with your mission as we commit and complement each other in striving to accomplish the goals and objectives bestowed on us by you.

Lord, let it be so.

Glory to you, O God.

Amen.

Created in collaboration with Jim Oehrig, Hope Rises International

For Reconciliation

O God of peace, help us be still.

Father God, we come before you seeking restoration in our hearts and relationships. Everything is a gift from you, who brought us back to you through Christ. And so you have given us, too, this task of reconciliation.[83]

For there is no other God like you,
who pardons us and overlooks our sins.
Lord, let us be like you.
You do not stay angry with your people forever,
because you delight in showing unfailing love.[84]
Lord, let us be like you.

Lord, guide us as we strive to heal broken bonds and foster unity. Grant us humility, patience, and grace to mend what has been fractured. Help us to be a reflection of your love and forgiveness in all our interactions, and may your peace reign in our lives.

Lord, make us instruments of your peace.
Let us sow love, truth, and pardon.
Let us not so much seek
to be consoled as to console;
to be understood as to understand;
to be loved as to love.
For it is in giving that we receive;
it is in pardoning that we are pardoned;
it is in self-forgetting that we find.[85]

Through the power of the Holy Spirit, let us do your good work of healing broken hearts and relationships, embodying the very reconciliation you have so freely given us through Christ Jesus.

Lord, hear our prayer.

Amen.

Created in collaboration with Pamela Armstrong-Pautz, Hope Rises International

LITURGIES FOR OUR
WORK IN THE WORLD

For the Effectiveness of Ministry

O God, we long to be your hands and your feet.

Lord, we are humbled by the ministry you have called us to at (Organization). May we approach this work full of gratitude, humility, and faith. We acknowledge our dependence on you in effectively carrying out our mission, and we give thanks to you Lord, for you are good.[86]

We give thanks to you, Lord, for you are good.

Lord, grant us wisdom, discernment, patience, and courage as we engage the work. Establish the work of our hands. Equip and strengthen our team, growing us in maturity and competence. Allow for fruitful partnerships and effective collaborations.

May the favor of the Lord rest upon us.

Lord, let this ministry serve as a channel of Christ's love to those we serve. If it be your will, grow this ministry and multiply the impact. May we seek to measure success by your kingdom values and give you the glory.

O Lord, we pray, give us success.

Hear our prayer.

Amen.

Created in collaboration with Melissa Edmiston, Hope Rises International

For the Proclamation of the Gospel

God, we long to sing of your love to the whole world.

We will tell all people about your justice.
We are not afraid to speak out,
as you, O Lord, well know.
We will not keep the good news hidden in our hearts;
We will speak of your faithfulness and saving power,
of your unfailing love and faithfulness.[87]

O Father, proclamation is easy to understand, but it is difficult to do.

May you fan the flame within us for gospel demonstration, creating spiritual curiosity in those around us.

Christ, have mercy.

Constantly feed the fire within us to make known the gospel, and for those around us to have ears to hear.

Lord, let it be so.

May our efforts, works, and words be always gospel centric, steeped in opportunities to communicate your grace, mercy, and love to those you have prepared to watch us, listen to us, engage with us, and walk with us.

Glory be to God, as it was in the beginning, is now, and ever shall be.

Amen.

Created in collaboration with Jim Oehrig, Hope Rises International

For Innovation and New Insights

Father, you are the Creator of the universe.

When we see the work of your fingers, we wonder:
What are mere mortals that you should think about them,
human beings that you should care for them?
Yet you have given us authority over this wondrous creation,[88]
and so we, too, create.

With a mere word, all of your creation came into being. We marvel at
your design and its intricate details, from the movement of celestial bodies
to the flow of minerals through cell walls. We humbly come before the
Author of all things as we seek to innovate and find new solutions to the
problems in our communities. The answer may be hidden from us at this
moment, but we pray that our eyes and ears would be open to what you
will reveal as we walk in the footsteps of our life-creating Father.

We know that Earth's crammed with heaven,
and every common bush afire with God.
In awe, we take off our shoes.[89]
We marvel at your creation.
We pray you guide as we seek to think like you.

Thank you as sons and daughters of the Most High King that we get to be a part of your kingdom coming on Earth as it is in heaven. We also humbly acknowledge that you knew about this challenge long before it even entered our minds, and you have prepared a path forward. Let us look back upon your provision and faithfulness as much as we look forward to what is yet to come.

Lord, hear our prayer.

Amen.

Created in collaboration with David Snyder, Sustainable Medical Missions

For the Renewing of Creation

Maker of the heavens and the earth, you set the stars in the sky!

For this we pray:
that the wolf will live with the lamb, the leopard with the goat,
the calf and the lion and the yearling safe together,
led by a little child.
That nothing will hurt or destroy
on all God's holy mountain,
for as the waters fill the sea
so the earth will be filled with people who know the Lord.[90]

Lord, Father, and King, you designed and created the cosmos. The tiny part
of it you entrusted to us suffers because of our unevenness and imbalances,
our brokenness and misplaced priorities, and our ill-placed emphasis on
the person in the mirror.

Forgive us, Lord, for misplacing our loyalties.

May you instill in us a yearning to see all of creation renewed, restored,
reconstituted, reviewed, and replenished.

Christ, have mercy.

May we become instruments in your hands to pursue this holiest of
causes—the *restoration of all things.*

Lord, hear our prayer.

Amen.

Created in collaboration with Jim Oehrig, Hope Rises International

For Vision

O God, your thoughts are higher than our thoughts, and your ways are higher than our ways.[91]

You have planted eternity in our hearts,
yet we cannot see or fathom the whole of your work.[92]
We praise you, most dear, most unknowable God.

The glimpses of your kingdom we have seen are compelling and beautiful, yet we know we see as if through a glass dimly.[93] *We long to see more clearly. We want to see your vision and how our work can bring your desires more tangibly into this world. We ask you for your vision for our organization that fits into your vision for the world and all its people.*

Grant us, O Lord, the grace to see. O Lord, give us your vision.

Christ, have mercy.

If what you show us seems too beautiful to imagine, grant us the grace to believe.

Lord, hear our prayer.

If what you reveal seems impossible, grant us the grace of faith. Show us what you will, O God, but then bring it into being through your grace. Grant us the courage to both follow and lead in the direction you are guiding toward the vision that you are giving. All this we ask for your sake; your kingdom come, your will be done.

Amen.

Created in collaboration with Bill Haley, Coracle

For Troubled Times

God has brought us here and is present with us. Let us pour out the confusion and grief that overwhelm us, with the assurance of God's presence in the midst of suffering.

Our God, we confess:
We have crossed outside of your will.
We have believed our own way of thinking is supreme.
We have not seen every human being as a child of God.
We have perpetrated harsh words and acted in cold indifference.
We have not received the stories and experiences of those different from ourselves.
We have pledged our allegiance to causes other than you.
We have not responded boldly to end bigotry, violence, and racism.
We have defended structures that benefit ourselves at the expense of others.
Lord, have mercy on us, a weak, broken, and fearful people.

God knows our hearts and hears the darkest confessions of our souls. The spirit of God rests upon the broken-hearted and repentant. Receive now God's forgiveness for you, a beautiful and loved child of God, even in the midst of all that is incomplete.

Our God, we pray for the love and strength to cross out of the boundaries we have created for our own comfort, peace, security, and privilege. As we go forth:
We seek your comfort—comfort in the midst of affliction.
We seek your peace—peace in the midst of violence.
We seek your security—security in the midst of chaos.
We seek the privilege you provide—the privilege to lay down our lives for others.

Lord, we follow you into a tumultuous world with hearts at rest in the knowledge of your presence, filled with your love, contending with you for all things to be made whole.

Amen.

Created in collaboration with Sami DiPasquale (Abara), from a prayer created by Coracle

For the Restoration of People's Dignity and Hope

God, our Father, we come to you on behalf of those who have been bruised and battered.

For you, Christ, comfort the broken-hearted,
free the prisoners,
bring good news to the poor.[94]

You have made each of your children in your divine image and placed in them the ability to reflect you to the world, but that reflection is lost and hidden in so many lives. We pray for those who, suffering shame, abandonment, isolation, and exclusion, have hidden themselves away from the world and, many times, from you.

We pray for those who groan all the day long,
their strength sapped as in the heat of summer.[95]

As we encounter those who suffer shame and hopelessness, with the loving care of your Son, Jesus Christ, may we extend to them words and works that restore to them their value and worth as human beings. Enable us to come alongside them and, with your help, see them walk with heads held high and your dignity restored within them. May they begin to see themselves as you see them and understand the depths of the riches which are theirs in you.

Help us, Lord.

In the name of the Father, the Son, and the Holy Spirit.

Amen.

Created by the author

For Sensitivity to Context and Culture

Almighty God, we glorify your name as we marvel at the diversity of your creation.

As we work across different continents and cultures, we ask that you grant us wisdom and humility.

Fill us with the knowledge of your will
through all the wisdom and understanding that the Spirit gives,
that we may bear fruit in this good work.[96]

Help us to see your handprints in the experiences, stories, and traditions of our partners and the people we serve.

Lord, let us show every partner, every community, and every person we encounter the same love, compassion, and grace that you show us. May our interactions be marked by mutual respect, collaboration, and appreciation.

Help us to be sensitive with our words, attitudes, and actions. Fill us with the spirit of Jesus Christ, who came not to be served but to serve.

May our work reflect the beautiful mosaic of your kingdom,
where every nation, tribe, people, and language shall stand before
the throne
and in front of the Lamb.[97]
We ask this in the name of Jesus Christ, our Lord.

Amen.

Created in collaboration with Deborah Mensah, Hope Rises International

For a Time of Challenge or Uncertainty

God, thank you for the opportunity to be in this time, in this place, with these people, with this mission.

As Mordecai reminded Esther:
Who knows but that we have come to where we are
for just such a time as this?[98]

We thank you for the privilege of being able to put the gifts you've given us to your service, here and now, and to apply our best efforts toward your purposes in this way. Right now, O Lord, it is hard. There are challenges we are facing, needs that we have, different paths to consider, and decisions to make. And so we ask you for wisdom.

Jesus, when they were tired and unsure, you gave your disciples ideas of how to do their work. You spoke to them.

We ask you to speak to us.

Lord, hear our prayer.

We ask you to guide our thinking by your spirit, grant us your ideas, and help us discern what is from you.

Lord, hear our prayer.

You are faithful, and we praise you.

We ask for your grace.

Amen.

Created in collaboration with Bill Haley, Coracle

LITURGIES FOR MISSION-SPECIFIC SERVICES AND MOMENTS

For the Dedication of a Well

God, fountain of living water, we praise and thank you.

O God, you are our God;
Our souls thirst for you;
our bodies long for you
in a parched and weary land.
Your unfailing love is better than life itself.
We will praise you as long as we live
with songs of joy.[99]

Lord, may this water flow, and may your blessing abound.

May we have struck water, but may we have not struck the rock, as Moses
did in his own strength and anger.[100] *For we, too, are so often lost in the*
wilderness[101] *as we wander through the unknown of this life on our way*
to paradise. We do have a frustration, for your people do not have water,
their throats are parched, and their lives are a struggle in this land. But
we know this is life outside of Eden, and despite the curse of sin, we rejoice
as you have poured forth waters in the desert, you have given us this well,
this spring of life, and above all, you have poured forth living water in
Christ, that we may never thirst again.[102]

Stir us, O God, when we have lost our thirst for the water of life.
When we have ceased to dream of eternity, allowed our vision of
heaven to grow dim,

Stir us again.
Draw us back to your water in joy and in hope.[103]

We celebrate you, the one who hid this water so deep beneath us in your creation. May this water flow forever, and may we taste our Lord with every sip of life that flows from this well to every member of the community, every day from this point forward, always; in his holy name.

Amen.

Created in collaboration with Matt Hangen, Water4

For Water, Sanitation, and Hygiene (WASH) Projects

We praise you, Creator God, for the gift of water that sustains and renews, for its life-giving power and for the cleanliness it brings to our bodies and our homes. We seek your blessing upon this much-needed project, that it may be a beacon.

Is anyone thirsty?
Come and drink—
even if you have no money!
Why pay for food that does you no good?
Listen to God, and you will eat what is good.
Come to God with your ears wide open.
Listen, and you will find life.[104]

Almighty God, who created the heavens and the earth and placed in our hands the stewardship of this world, grant us wisdom and compassion as we care for the resources you have given us, especially the water that sustains our lives. May we use it wisely, keep it pure, and share it freely, so that all may benefit from its abundance.

For the gift of water, that it may be pure, plentiful, and available to all people, we pray to you, O Lord.

Lord, hear our prayer.

For our donors and all who work to provide clean water, sanitation, and hygiene education in our communities, that they may be strengthened in their labors and supported by our prayers, we pray to you, O Lord.

Lord, hear our prayer.

For those who suffer from waterborne diseases and lack of sanitation, that they may be healed and that we may be moved to help alleviate their suffering, we pray to you, O Lord.

Lord, hear our prayer.

For our community, that we may use water wisely, maintain cleanliness, and teach the importance of hygiene to our children, we pray to you, O Lord.

Lord, hear our prayer.

May the God who created the waters bless and keep us. May Christ, the living water, refresh our souls. May the Holy Spirit guide us in the care of God's creation, that we may go forth to serve our community in love and peace.

Lord, let your presence be upon us.

Amen.

Created in collaboration with Mike Mantel
and the global staff of Living Water International

For the Dedication of an Airplane

God, use this craft for your good work.

You give power to the weak
and strength to the powerless.
Even youths will become weak and tired,
and young men will fall in exhaustion.
But those who trust in the Lord will find new strength.
They will soar high on wings like eagles.[105]

Father, we acknowledge that all good things come from you. Today we dedicate this aircraft to serve your kingdom. We're grateful for the generosity of those who have made it possible for us to acquire and equip it. We celebrate the many people who are collectively serving together so that this airplane can reach those living in isolation.

My Lord, fill this empty vessel with love, faith, and treasures
that it may be used for your good work.

Knowing the challenging environment that awaits this craft, we ask for your protection for our pilots and passengers. And we pray for those who will be impacted by the flights it will make, flights that will bring needed supplies and transportation. May this airplane serve as a symbol of your love for them, helping them to see that they are not forgotten. And may that awareness of your love bring needed change in their lives, drawing them closer to you.

Lord, hear our prayer.

Amen.

Created in collaboration with David Holsten, Mission Aviation Fellowship

For the Victims of Human Trafficking

Lord, you never forget any of your children; their cries are ever before you.

O Lord, you know us all:
when we sit and when we stand,
when we travel and rest.
You know our every thought.
You go before us and follow us.
You place your hand of blessing on each head.[106]

You see, know, and remember the child trapped in a brothel, deep in a place where it seems that nobody can find her. You know her name; you hold her in your arms. She is not lost to you. According to the cross, she is the most valuable person in the world.

You are the hero of each story,
and we are transformed by your Holy Spirit and Word.
You are the rescuer
and the redeemer,
not us.
Even as we join in your work,
it is your intervention we need.

We humbly admit that the brokenness of this world is far beyond our power to heal, but you are the God who moves mountains, and you are among us. You are the one who walks into the darkest cave to deliver the prisoners from their chains. You are the one who sees deep into the truth of our past only to speak into the brightest future. You are the one who extends life and healing to the blighted, the weak, the rejected, and the optionless.

We do not lose hope.
We cling to you, our hope.
You are actively redeeming all things from above and within.
Let your child not lose hope in her suffering;
let us not lose heart in the pursuit;
for you have already written a new story,
an eternal one that celebrates every unforgotten, suffering human soul.

Christ, be with us all.

Amen.

Created in collaboration with Mike Mercer, Compassion First

For Encountering Trauma

O Lord, you are strong: infinite, all-powerful, untouched by evil. O Lord, you are loving: kind, understanding, providing comfort to the broken-hearted.

Rise up, O God.
Give justice to the poor and the orphans.
Uphold the rights of the oppressed,
rescue the helpless,[107]
bind the wounds of those who sorrow.[108]
You are dangerous to the wicked,
and endlessly safe and accepting of those who hide in the shelter of your wings.

We choose to wrap ourselves in the safety and comfort of your presence, to let your strength and love enclose us and carry us for what we will hear and see today.

We carry your light within us into this dark space.
Darkness cannot overcome you.

Tender and merciful Christ, be with us.

May we listen with compassion and understanding;
may we be quick to demonstrate help and support,
and slow to speak when words are not needed.

May we see with eyes of mercy the beauty of the soul you created,
even now through the recounted story of pain, cruelty, injustice, and loss.

May we feel with appropriate empathy the sorrow, anger, and fear that trauma creates,
and yet let not those emotions take up residence in our own hearts.

Lord, hear our prayer.

Give us, O Lord, a place to stand;
a rock that is higher than we are[109] amid the chaos.

We claim your hope as a helmet and shield. By your spirit, we ask you to guard our hearts, reminding us that we are safe, accepted, and enough in you,
even in the face of the pain, violence, injustice, and suffering that we encounter today.

We carry your light into this dark,
and trust that your transforming power can work through us.

Glory be to God.

Amen.

Created in collaboration with Lisa Ramsey, CAMA Services,

The Christian and Missionary Alliance

For Disaster Response

Lord, can you not hear the earth crying out for rescue?

Why have you hidden your face from us?[110]

Even Moses asked, "Why?"
Even Habakkuk,
Even the disciples.
Even Christ himself.
O God, our God, why have you forsaken us?[111]

We lament in one voice.

We strive to be your hands and feet, but Lord, we are overrun by daily
catastrophes.
We stand in this faithful tradition of asking, "Why?"
We plead with you in the company of all your saints,
and that brings a strange solace.

Lord, we long to be counted amongst those who not only cry
out, "Why?"
but also continue to fight for justice.
Do not let us grow weary in doing good.
Let us draw near to your faithful presence that is so powerfully felt
among the suffering.
Let us pursue you in the midst of our "Why?"

May your followers find the grace and boldness to see you in the midst of the chaos. May we find our center in you, the eye of the storm.

Amen.

Created in collaboration with Jake Stum,
Anglican Relief and Development Fund

For the Shipment of Medicine and Vaccines

O God, we call to you from the depths of our hearts.

You will rescue the poor when they cry;
God, help the oppressed, who have no one to defend them.
Rescue the weak and the needy,
Redeem their precious lives.[112]

For the one crying out from an orphanage in South Korea, the one afflicted
with polio, the disabled child viciously mocked, the one who is told they
are being punished for their parents' sin: O God, have mercy upon them.
O Lord, hear our cry.

All are loved by God and created in his image.
We are God's workmanship created in Christ Jesus to do good works
which he prepared in advance for us to do.[113]
You call us to look after the sick, O God.

Let lifesaving medicines and vaccines reach the whole world.
Lord, may your grace, mercy, and love move us to action.

Amen.

Created in collaboration with Steve Stirling, MAP International

ACKNOWLEDGMENTS

WRITING A BOOK of any length seemed a daunting task. Through the encouragement and help of many people, I have crossed this first bridge—and I hope it will not be the last. It was not a solo act, and I would like to thank those who have enabled this work to see the light of day.

"Thank you" is not enough to say, but alas, it is the phrase we have. I want to thank:

- My children, without whom I would not have learned the way of brokenness and the redemption of rest.
- My wife Cindi, who is my biggest fan and is the person I most want to be like when I grow up.
- My sons Seth, Jacob, and Eli, and my daughter Ahna. My pursuit of Christ has been shaped by a desire to be a better father to each of you. And thanks to my son Seth, whose art captures the soul of my sabbatical experience in a way words cannot.
- Sarah Hesshaus, for your constant support and encouragement of my writing over the years.

- Janiece Robinson, for teaching me the structure and discipline of storytelling.
- Philip Yancey, for our chats on writing, and on neglected diseases like leprosy.
- Hallie Knox, for jumping right in and saying yes. Your influence on my words and ideas are golden.
- Tom Dean, for your guidance and counsel which suddenly made it all become a reality.
- Bill Haley, for your companionship and mystical challenge to pursue the God who is love.
- Ken Wilson, for affirming my pursuit of this goal.
- Pam Armstrong-Pautz, for your words at a critical moment, urging me out into the publishing abyss.
- The brothers at Christ in the Desert, who model a way of living and gospel proclamation that have become indelible in my life.
- All those CEOs and leaders who contributed prayers to shape our "shared liturgy."
- The staff at my organization (many of whom contributed prayers included in this book), for enabling this CEO to call us into a new way of being together.
- And my board of directors, who have given me the support and freedom to fully follow God and his direction.

So many friends and family have played a role in this journey; I will have to thank each of you in person so you know how deeply I mean it.

It is my prayer that this is the beginning of many needed thanks in the future. May God be so gracious.

Hallie Knox was a great writing companion to me in this process. If you need someone who can help you get your ideas onto a page, contact her on LinkedIn at Hallie Knox, Freelance Writer or by email at h.anne.knox@gmail.com.

ENDNOTES

1. Also known as Policy Governance® and created by Dr. John Carver, boards using this model focus on the overarching policies (the "ends") rather than the daily operations (the "means") within an organization. You can learn more at http://www.carvergovernance.com.
2. The word "Psalter" refers simply to a collection of the Psalms in one book, for liturgical use and personal prayer.
3. Attributed.
4. Henri Nouwen, *The Way of the Heart* (New York: HarperOne, 2009), 6.
5. St. Benedict spoke to the structure and importance of the Divine Office in his most loved and influential work, *The Rule of Saint Benedict*.
6. Dietrich Bonhoeffer, *Life Together: The Classic Exploration of Christian Community* (New York: HarperOne, 2009), 97.
7. More information can be found at http://www.thelightphone.com.
8. Luke 8:45.
9. Mark 5:31.

10. Dallas Willard, *The Divine Conspiracy: Rediscovering Our Hidden Life in God* (New York: Harper, 1998), 95.

11. Mark 10:14.

12. Luke 19:1–10.

13. Marc A. Russo, Danielle M. Santarelli, Dean O'Rourke, "The Physiological Effects of Slow Breathing in the Healthy Human," *Breathe* 13 (2017): 298–309, https://doi.org/10.1183/20734735.009817.

14. Andrea Zaccaro et al., "How Breath-Control Can Change Your Life: A Systematic Review on Psycho-Physiological Correlates of Slow Breathing," *Frontiers of Human Neuroscience*, 06 September 2018, Sec. Brain Health and Clinical Neuroscience, Volume 12—2018.

15. 2 Corinthians 10:5.

16. Brother Lawrence, *The Practice of the Presence of God* (UK: Spire, 1967), 79–80.

17. Thomas Merton, *Contemplative Prayer* (New York: Image, 1971), 67.

18. Quoted in Pope St. Pius X's 1911 Apostolic Constitution, *Divini Afflatu*, from "Letter of St. Athanasius, Archbishop of Alexandria, to Marcellinus, Concerning the Psalms," https://www.livefatima.io/letter-of-st-athanasius-archbishop-of-alexandria-to-marcellinus-concerning-the-psalms/.

19. Nouwen, *The Way of the Heart*, 28.

20. Tom Wright, *Finding God in the Psalms* (London: SPCK Publishing, 2014), 6.

21. Henry David Thoreau, *Walden; or, Life in the Woods* (Walden Pond: Internet Bookmobile, 2004), 159.

22. Martin Luther, *A Simple Way to Pray* (Milwaukee: Northwestern Publishing House, 2017), 1.

23. Nouwen, *The Way of the Heart*, 82.

24. Thomas R. Kelly, *A Testament of Devotion* (New York: HarperOne, 1996), 8.
25. G. K. Chesterton, *Orthodoxy* (Project Gutenburg: 2021).
26. John Calvin, *Commentary on Psalms* (Grand Rapids: Christian Classics Ethereal Library), 23.
27. Kelly, *A Testament of Devotion*, 5.
28. A doxology is defined as being a short, liturgical hymn of praise to God, from the Greek *doxa-* (glory) and *-logos* (speaking).
29. John 10:30.
30. Psalm 23:5.
31. Adapted from Psalm 145:1–7.
32. Adapted from the Lord's Prayer, Matthew 6:9–13.
33. Matthew 6:25–34.
34. Adapted from Psalm 23.
35. Psalm 23:1.
36. Psalm 145:15–18.
37. Adapted from the Orthodox Akathist Hymn, Glory to God for All Things (also called the Akathist of Thanksgiving), https://www.saintjonah.org/services/thanksgiving.htm.
38. Proverbs 2:1–7.
39. Adapted from Emily Dickinson's poem "The Brain—is wider than the Sky," https://viva.pressbooks.pub/amlit1/chapter/the-brain-is-wider-than-the-sky-ca-1858-1865-emily-dickinson/.
40. Adapted from Psalm 147.
41. Proverbs 16:3.
42. Psalm 90:17.
43. Isaiah 52:7.
44. Isaiah 43:2.
45. Adapted from "Saint Patrick's Breastplate," https://en.wikipedia.org/wiki/Saint_Patrick%27s_Breastplate.
46. Adapted from 1 Peter 4:10.
47. Psalm 103:1–5.

48. Ephesians 3:20.
49. Psalm 106:1–3.
50. Isaiah 43:19.
51. Adapted from Psalm 90.
52. Psalm 127:1.
53. Adapted from Marge Piercy, "To Be of Use," *To Be of Use: Poems by Marge Piercy* (Doubleday, 1973).
54. Genesis 1:28; 9:1.
55. Genesis 1:4–31.
56. Adapted from Psalm 33.
57. Mark 4:30–32.
58. Psalm 62:1–2.
59. Adapted from Wendell Berry, "Sabbath," *This Day: Collected & New Sabbath Poems* (Counterpoint, 2013).
60. Exodus 34:29–30.
61. Adapted from Psalm 139:13–16.
62. Psalm 127:3.
63. Matthew 23:37.
64. Adapted from C. S. Lewis, "Love's as Warm as Tears," *Poems* (Mariner Books, 2002).
65. Deuteronomy 31:8.
66. Psalm 37: 3–5.
67. Isaiah 30:21.
68. Adapted from Ecclesiastes 3:1–8.
69. Adapted from Alicia Ostriker, "The Blessing of the Old Woman, the Tulip, and the Dog," *The Book of Seventy* (University of Pittsburgh Press, 2009).
70. Numbers 6:24–26.
71. 2 Corinthians 13:14.
72. Adapted from Psalm 145:1–3.
73. Matthew 20:28.
74. 1 Corinthians 15:58.

75. Psalm 24:1–2.
76. Psalm 78:72.
77. Psalm 133:2.
78. Micah 6:8.
79. Isaiah 64:8.
80. Ecclesiastes 4:12.
81. 1 Corinthians 12:12–26.
82. Exodus 17:11–12.
83. 2 Corinthians 5:18.
84. Micah 7:18.
85. Adapted from the prayer of Saint Francis, https://www.catholic. org/prayers/prayer.php?p=134.
86. Psalm 107:1.
87. Psalm 40:9–10.
88. Psalm 8:3–9.
89. Adapted from a line in Elizabeth Barrett Browning's poem "Aurora Leigh," https://www.bartleby.com/lit-hub/the-oxfor d-book-of-english-mystical-verse/86-from-aurora-leigh/.
90. Adapted from Isaiah 11.
91. Isaiah 55:8.
92. Ecclesiastes 3:11.
93. 1 Corinthians 13:12.
94. Isaiah 6:11.
95. Psalm 32:4.
96. Colossians 1:9–10.
97. Revelation 7:9.
98. Esther 4:14.
99. Adapted from Psalm 63:1–5.
100. Numbers 20:10–13.
101. Joshua 5:6.
102. John 4:14.

103. Adapted from "Disturb Us, Lord," a prayer attributed to Sir Francis Drake, https://renovare.org/articles/disturb-us-lord.

104. Adapted from Isaiah 55:1–3.

105. Isaiah 40:30–31.

106. Adapted from Psalm 139.

107. Psalm 146:7.

108. Psalm 147:3.

109. Psalm 61:2.

110. Psalm 44:24.

111. Psalm 22:1.

112. Adapted from Psalm 72:12–14.

113. Ephesians 2:10.

ABOUT THE AUTHOR

BILL HAS BEEN a CEO of national and international organizations in the for-profit and nonprofit world for well over two decades. Since
2010 he has served as President and CEO of Hope Rises International,
which was founded in 1906. He has been blessed to lead many boards
and organizations around the world and most recently began serving
as chair of the board for the Accord Network. His experience running
Christian ministry organizations for his entire career, coupled with
a life-altering three-month sabbatical experience a few years ago, has
shaped his desire to write and think about the role of spiritual formation in Christian parachurch ministries. Bill and his wife Cindi live
in Greenville, SC, where they attend the Village Church Anglican
and delight in their teenage daughter, three adult children, and three
grandchildren. Bill graduated from the University of Tennessee with a
BA in Political Science and is pursuing postgraduate work in spiritual
formation at Gordon–Conwell Theological Seminary.

If you want to receive the daily reading plan in your inbox, scan the QR code below and you can sign up. Or go to www.billsimmons.net and find all the ways you can engage with this content by yourself or with a group.

Hope Rises
INTERNATIONAL
Formerly American Leprosy Missions

Discover the redemptive work being done with and through the church to serve people around the world with neglected tropical diseases like leprosy.

Hope Rises International believes that as Christians, we are called to make disciples. We know that faith in Christ is the only path to experiencing life to the fullest—it's what we were created for. Everyone needs the good news of the gospel. This conviction is the driving force in everything we do serving people suffering from pain, disability, isolation and stigma caused by neglected tropical diseases (NTDs).

Founded as American Leprosy Missions in 1906, Hope Rises International is a parachurch ministry that partners with faith leaders, congregations, and Christian hospitals who are:

+ finding people suffering from NTDs
+ referring suspected cases for diagnosis and care
+ ensuring access to quality treatment
+ teaching critical self-care practices
+ providing ongoing disease management
+ offering spiritual and emotional support
+ supporting community development

Hope Rises International proudly works with Christian partners serving people affected by neglected tropical diseases around the world

When we come alongside the local church to care for suffering people and share the gospel as we go, bodies heal. Souls heal. **And hope rises**.

Learn more about our ministry, our Christian partners, and the people we serve as we continue joining Jesus in His redemptive work.

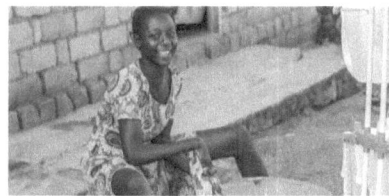

One Alm Way | Greenville, SC 29601 | (800) 543-3135 | HopeRises.org